P9-DBT-440

PEOPLE
to
KNOW
TODAY

ROBERT FROST
The Life of America's Poet

Sara McIntosh Wooten

Enslow Publishers, Inc.
40 Industrial Road
Box 398
Berkeley Heights, NJ 07922
USA
http://www.enslow.com

Library of Congress Cataloging-in-Publication Data

Wooten, Sara McIntosh.
    Robert Frost : the life of America's poet / by Sara McIntosh Wooten.
        p. cm. – (People to know today)
    Includes bibliographical references and index.
    ISBN 0-7660-2627-2
    [1. Frost, Robert, 1874–1963.—Juvenile literature. 2. Poets, American—
20th century—Biography—Juvenile literature.] I. Title. II. Series.
    PS3511.R94Z994 2006
    811'.52—dc22   2005034882

Printed in the United States of America

10 9 8 7 6 5 4 3 2 1

To Our Readers: We have done our best to make sure all Internet Addresses in this book were active
and appropriate when we went to press. However, the author and the publisher have no control over
and assume no liability for the material available on those Internet sites or on other Web sites they may
link to. Any comments or suggestions can be sent by e-mail to comments@enslow.com or to the
address on the back cover.

Every effort has been made to locate all copyright holders of material used in this book. If any
errors or omissions have occurred, corrections will be made in future editions of this book.

"Bereft" and "Stopping by Woods on a Snowy Evening" from
THE POETRY OF ROBERT FROST edited by Edward Connery Lathem.
Copyright 1923, 1928, 1969 by Henry Holt and Company. Copyright 1951, 1956 by Robert Frost.
Reprinted by permission of Henry Holt and Company, LLC

Illustration Credits: AP/Wide World, pp. 34, 48, 66, 89TL, 100; Robert Frost Collection,
Clifton Waller Barrett Library of American Literature, Special Collections, University of
Virginia Library, pp. 15, 22, 29, 43, 55, 57, 70, 75, 76, 79, 84, 89B, 89R; Courtesy of
Dartmouth College Library, pp. 13 (both), 16, 26, 63; Library of Congress, pp. 32, 45, 59,
105; Time Life Pictures/Getty Images, pp. 1, 4, 8, 81, 91, 95, 103, 107.

Cover Photograph: Time Life Pictures/Getty Images

CONTENTS

TIME

THE WEEKLY NEWSMAGAZINE

Boris Chaliapin

POET ROBERT FROST
"Good fences make good neighbors."
(Books)

Robert Frost had become one of the most-loved poets in America.

1
A GIFT FOR THE NATION

The sun shone brightly on that frosty January day in 1961. A thick blanket of fresh snow covered the ground. Thousands of people in Washington, D.C., waited patiently in the cold for the inauguration of America's thirty-fifth president, John F. Kennedy. At the same time, millions of viewers across the nation were ready to watch the ceremony on television.

The speakers that day were seated on a central platform, each waiting to take part in the ceremony. Among them was the American poet Robert Frost.

By this time, the eighty-six-year-old Frost had become well known to most adults in America. More than likely, many of them had studied his poetry in school and were familiar with his style of writing. Frost used straightforward, simple language to describe nature and ordinary life in new and fresh ways. He had written thirteen books of poetry and had received an unprecedented four Pulitzer Prizes for his work. He had also been awarded more than forty honorary degrees from colleges and universities in the United States and England, and his life and work had been featured as the cover story for the October 9, 1950, edition of *Time* magazine.

President-elect Kennedy was pleased to have Frost speak at his inaugural.[1] He had personally requested the presence of the aging poet on this special day. It was the first time in United States history that a poet would speak at a presidential inauguration.

Kennedy was well acquainted with Frost's work. In fact, during his presidential campaign, he had ended campaign speeches with the poet's words, "I have miles to go before I sleep," taken from one of Frost's best-known and beloved poems, "Stopping by Woods on a Snowy Evening."

In planning for Frost's presentation, Kennedy had asked Frost to create a special poem to read that day. Even though the request came from the president-elect, Frost was not

The President-Elect

At age forty-four, John F. Kennedy was the youngest United States president. During his term of office, he became best known for ordering a naval blockade of Cuba in 1962, which led to the removal of Soviet nuclear missiles from Cuba. He was assassinated before the end of his third year in office.

intimidated. Still, he declined the challenge because he was uncomfortable writing poems on demand.[2]

As January 20 approached, however, Frost relented and began working on a new poem for the occasion. It would be entitled "Dedication" (later renamed "For John F. Kennedy His Inauguration"). While not considered one of Frost's best works, "Dedication" was appropriate in content and message for the event. Frost planned to read it first, then follow it with another of his poems, "The Gift Outright."

The inaugural ceremony began as scheduled, despite the bitter cold. Catholic Cardinal Richard Cushing spoke first, offering an opening prayer. Then Marian Anderson, the acclaimed African-American contralto, sang the national anthem. Shortly after that, Lyndon B. Johnson was sworn in as vice president.

Just before the most important part of the ceremony, when the president-elect would take his oath of office, Robert Frost slowly made his way to the podium. Bundled in a heavy gray overcoat, with his untamed white hair flowing, the great poet carried several pieces of paper in his hand. Not to be hurried, he carefully laid his work on the podium. Then he began to read his poem "Dedication" for the first time in public.

Instead of speaking confidently, Frost's words were halting and unsure. He seemed confused.[3] Soon the audience heard puzzling words from the speaker over

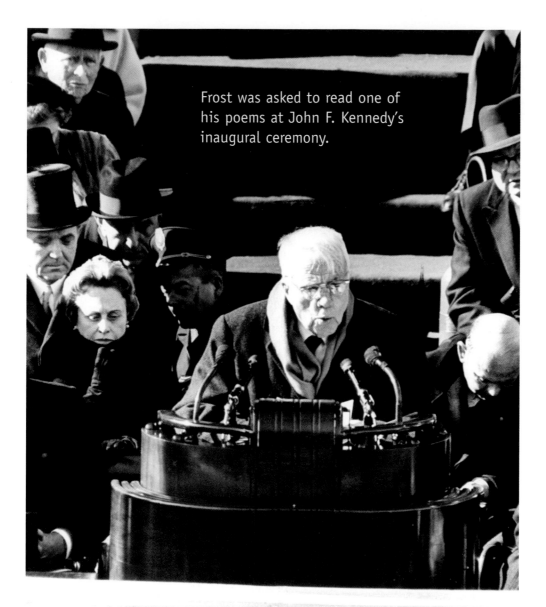

Frost was asked to read one of his poems at John F. Kennedy's inaugural ceremony.

the public address system: "No, I'm not having a good light here at all."[4] The glare of the sun on the paper his poem was written on made it impossible for him to read it. People in the audience, to show support for the elderly poet, clapped their encouragement.

Recognizing the problem, Vice President Johnson quickly stepped to the podium to try to shield the sun with his top hat. But Frost waved him off. Despite the formality and importance of the occasion, he was not concerned.[5] Instead of continuing with "Dedication," Frost quickly changed plans. In a strong, sure voice, he confidently began to recite from memory "The Gift Outright," one of his most popular poems.[6] He had written it twenty-six years earlier. It was published in 1942, just after the United States had entered World War II. Beginning with the words "The land was ours before we were the land's," Frost recited the poem with quiet dignity. With its patriotic theme—America's quest for independence from England—the dramatic poem held the audience's attention.

As Frost came to the end of the poem, the crowd broke into applause and cheered—not only for the poem but for the poet, who was considered by this time in his life to be one of America's most beloved and respected poets.[7]

Frost recited the poem with quiet dignity.

Frost sat down, having pulled off a grand and memorable performance despite an uncertain beginning. President-elect Kennedy was then sworn in as president. The next day, *The Washington Post* contained a story about the inaugural ceremony. It began, "Robert Frost in his natural way stole the hearts of the Inaugural crowd."[8] Frost had once more confirmed his place in America's heart. But his success as a poet had been a long time in coming.

> "Robert **Frost in his natural** way stole the **hearts** of the **Inaugural crowd.**"

His was a story of courage and the determination to hold on to a dream despite all obstacles.

2
THE WILD WEST

Robert Lee Frost was born on March 26, 1874, in San Francisco, California. It was just nine years after the Civil War, and he was named in honor of the Confederate general Robert E. Lee, whom his father admired. His father, William Prescott Frost Jr., called Will, was a reporter for the *San Francisco Daily Evening Bulletin*. His mother, Isabelle Moodie Frost, was a teacher.

Will Frost was a brash and impulsive man with a strong personality. Tall and handsome, he had dark hair, heavy sideburns, a mustache, and deep blue eyes. Growing up across the continent in Lawrence, Massachusetts, Will had been a challenge for his parents as a boy. He was often in trouble and paid no attention to his parents' rules.

As a young man, Will attended Harvard University, graduating with honors. Even then he had a reputation as an undisciplined sort, known for his drinking, gambling, and carrying on with women. As his son, Robert, would say years later, he was "a bad boy who never stopped being one."[1]

Upon graduation, Will decided to move to California. In Lawrence he felt restrained from doing as he pleased under the strict expectations of the New England culture and the critical eyes of his parents. He thought he might fit in better out west, where rules were few and life was more exciting.[2]

Running out of money on his way to California, Will stopped in Lewistown, Pennsylvania, to find work. He was hired as a school principal at Lewistown Academy, a small private school. The only other teacher at the academy was a young woman named Isabelle Moodie.

Isabelle, or Belle as she was called, had been born in Scotland. When she was twelve, she was sent to the United States to live with relatives in Columbus, Ohio. As an adult she taught math for several years in Columbus. Later, she took the teaching job offered at the Lewistown Academy.

Frost and Moodie had very different personalities. While he was bold and used to doing as he pleased, she was quiet and reserved and had a strong religious faith. Yet the couple shared a love of literature, and their

relationship blossomed despite their differences. They were married on March 18, 1873. In June, after the

The poet's parents: William Prescott Frost and Isabelle (Belle) Moodie Frost.

school term was over, they left Pennsylvania for San Francisco.

It did not take long for Will Frost to establish himself in the busy city. He found a job at the *Daily Evening Bulletin* and a small apartment on Washington Street. By mid-November 1873, Belle was pregnant with their first child.

Just a year after their marriage, Robert Frost, called Robbie, was born. With the new pressures of having a family, Will resorted to his old ways. He began drinking heavily, a habit that would continue for the rest of his life. He often left his wife and son in the evenings to drink with his friends. When he came home, the alcohol easily turned his mood sour, causing him to fly into a rage with his wife or child. Angry shouting and sometimes physical abuse resulted. On several occasions, Belle grabbed Robbie and went to a neighbor's house for safety.

Belle maintained her strong religious ties as a form of comfort and support in trying to deal with her husband's behavior. She became active at the Swedenborgian Church near their home. She took her son to church each Sunday, while her husband usually had an excuse that prevented him from attending services.[3] Despite the newness of their marriage, the couple's differences were pulling them apart.

During the eleven years the Frosts were in San Francisco, they lived in a number of different places. Belle preferred hotels, as she did not like to cook and keep house. But her husband quickly tired of the cramped quarters, and would move his family to a small house or apartment.[4] With Will's volatile behavior and the family's frequent moves, little Robbie grew up in a house of turmoil and uncertainty.[5]

In 1875, Will Frost left the *Evening Bulletin* for the *Daily Evening Post*, where he took over as city editor.

The Wild West

San Francisco in 1873 was a frontier town, full of excitement and opportunity. The city was bustling and growing quickly. The gold discovered nearby in 1848 had brought people streaming into the area by the thousands. With a steadily growing population, other industries sprang up as well, including railroads, ranching, banking, and iron mining.

Six-month-old Robbie Frost.

His career was going well. Along with his interest in journalism, he had high hopes of a career in politics. As a devoted Democrat, he began to work with the local Democratic Party, assisting with campaigns.

By the summer of 1876, Belle was so unhappy in her marriage that she decided to leave her husband, even though she was expecting their second child. Using the excuse of introducing her son to her husband's parents, Belle took Robbie, who was two years old, and left San Francisco for Massachusetts. She hoped to find refuge there.

Will's parents, however, were not pleased to have Belle and their grandson as guests. They thought Belle

should be with her husband.[6] Still, they let her remain with them for a time, and she gave birth to a daughter, Jeanie Florence, while there, on June 25, 1876.

Belle and her husband exchanged many letters that summer. He was filled with apologies for his behavior and wanted her to return. By the fall of 1876, she was back

Robbie and his baby sister, Jeanie.

in San Francisco to give the marriage another chance. Belle knew that her husband's health was bad. He had been diagnosed with consumption, a bacterial infection that usually attacks the lungs. It is now called tuberculosis. At that time there was no cure for the disease, and it was often fatal.

When he was five years old, Robbie began school at a private kindergarten a few blocks from his home. He had grown into a frail, fair-skinned little boy with blond hair and large blue eyes. He quickly found that school was not to his liking.[7] In unfamiliar surroundings and without his mother, Robbie became physically ill with stomach cramps. By his second day, he felt too sick to go back to school. The pattern continued day after day, so Belle decided to keep him home and teach him herself.

As the years passed, life in the Frost home became more and more upsetting. Will continued to drink very heavily. His drinking, together with his temper, made for a dangerous mix. Once he came home from work and found Robbie and a friend making a boat in the living room. Will became furious because of the mess, and he smashed the boat to pieces. Sometimes he even hit his son. Still, the young boy adored his father, whom he saw as "brave, strong, and enduring."[8] "I wanted to please my father," Robert Frost later said. "Nothing else much mattered."[9]

As Robbie grew older, he became involved with a

group of boys called the Washington Street Gang. They were led by a tall, streetwise boy named Seth Balso. Eager to be part of the gang, Robbie confronted Seth to ask if he could join. Seth wanted to know how tough Robbie was, so Robbie agreed to fight a boy standing nearby. That was not good enough for Seth, who insisted that Robbie fight two boys instead of just one. The fight began, and all three boys got roughed up before Seth finally stopped them. Robbie found himself with a split lip, a bloody nose, and some scrapes and bruises. Having proved his courage, he earned membership in the gang.

After his initiation, Robbie stole for the gang from time to time. Once he swiped new wheels for Seth's wagon, which was used as a go-cart. Another time he made off with a pig, which the boys sold in Chinatown. Robbie was slowly overcoming some of the insecurity and fear he had felt in his younger years.

All the while, Will Frost's health continued to decline. Yet he continued to think he could overcome his illness with alcohol and intense physical activity. An athletic man, he insisted on performing physical feats that he thought would increase his strength and beat the disease. Several times Will insisted on swimming far out into San Francisco Bay, leaving

Robbie was overcoming some of the insecurity and fear of his younger years.

Robbie on the shore to stand guard over his coat and his bottle of whiskey. These long swims terrified Robbie as he watched his father fade into the distance. He was afraid that his father would drown.[10] Although Will always managed to swim back to shore, these attempts to cure his illness just weakened him further.

As a result of his hard work for the Democratic Party, Will Frost was nominated to run for city tax collector in 1884. To help his dad, Robbie handed out flyers on street corners. With the expectation of winning, Will resigned his position at the *Post* so that he would be ready to take on his new duties for the city.

To his dismay and disappointment, Will lost the election. His defeat sent him into a deep depression. In addition to being devastated by his defeat, he was also out of a job.

Although he was soon hired by another paper, the *Daily Report*, his tuberculosis had gotten so bad that he was often too weak to work. He died on May 5, 1885, at the age of thirty-four, leaving his family penniless.

Will Frost's final request was to be buried back in Lawrence, Massachusetts. His parents sent money for the family to return to Massachusetts by train. Robbie Frost was eleven years old. Years later he remembered his grief over his father's death, saying, "I never spoke of my father for years after he went: I couldn't."[11]

3

A CHANGE OF SCENERY

Although the father he loved dearly was now dead, Robbie would feel his father's influence throughout his life. Robbie, or Rob as he was called as he grew older, would be filled with a desire to succeed and excel at whatever he tried. He would also carry forward his father's love of sports.

The Frost family made the long journey across the country by train from San Francisco to Lawrence. They arrived at Grandfather Frost's home on 370 Haverhill Street in late spring 1885. A second funeral service for Will Frost was held there, after which his body was laid to rest at Bellevue Cemetery.

Formal and reserved by nature, Grandfather Frost was a well-respected man in the Lawrence community. He worked as a foreman in a local textile mill and was known and admired for his thriftiness with money.

He and his wife made space for their daughter-in-law and her two children in two small rooms on the third floor of their home. The rooms on the second floor were kept vacant so that they could be rented out if a tenant appeared.

Robbie would feel his father's influence throughout his life.

In contrast with Belle's more nurturing and motherly ways, the elder Frosts lived a highly disciplined life. They were not happy to have to take in their son's family and did not approve of the way Belle was raising their grandchildren. They thought she should be stricter with them.[1]

That fall Belle and her children moved out of Grandfather Frost's home, renting two small rooms in an apartment building in Lawrence. Rob and Jeanie began school. Upon taking examinations to determine which grades they should be placed in, Jeanie began in fourth grade while Rob, much to his dismay, started in third grade.[2] As the school year progressed, Jeanie did very well, while her brother floundered.

Once again Rob hated school. For one thing, he was still having great difficulty with reading. Frustrated, he refused to do some of his assignments. At one point, a stressed Mrs. Frost confided to a friend that her son, like his father, was stubborn and quick-tempered.[3]

Robbie

Mrs. Frost

Robbie was in his mother's class when she taught in Salem, New Hampshire.

Shortly afterward, in the winter of 1886, Belle found a teaching position in nearby Salem, New Hampshire, about ten miles from Lawrence. She was hired to teach a class of thirty-four children. Taught in one classroom, the students ranged from fifth- to eighth-grade. Rob and Jeanie were included in her class as fifth graders. Once she was hired, Belle moved her family into a boardinghouse near the railroad depot in Salem.

Mrs. Frost's job did not pay very well, and the family's finances were strained. As her son said years later, " . . . it [his mother's pay] sort of kept soul and body together—sort of."[4] Rob would help by picking up odd jobs over the next few years while he lived at home.

While Rob continued to struggle in school, he found a happy diversion in playing baseball, a sport he became very good at. A competitive player, he was an excellent pitcher. He would continue to enjoy playing baseball well into his middle age. Although his career goals changed as he grew older, at this time in his life Rob imagined himself as a major league pitcher.

As her children grew up, Mrs. Frost kept up her longtime habit of reading to them at home. Rob's favorite book was *Tom Brown's School Days*, by Thomas Hughes. He enjoyed the book so much that he would not let his mother finish it, because he did not want the story to end.[5] After they read this book, Rob was inspired for the first time to try harder in school.[6]

Deciding to move from the boardinghouse, the Frosts next rented rooms in the farmhouse of Mr. and Mrs. Loren Bailey. Mr. Bailey was a farmer, but he also had a side business making shoes. Before long, he hired Rob to help assemble shoes during his off-hours from school.

Over time, Rob's reading skills improved and he became more successful with his school assignments. But it was not until he was fourteen that Rob finally became a competent reader.[7] Mrs. Bailey lent him her copy of *The Scottish Chiefs*, by Jane Porter. This historical novel fascinated Rob. It was the first book he ever read all the way through by himself.

Mrs. Frost was considered a good teacher by most. She used teaching methods that were unusual for that time, such as grouping students by their abilities rather than by their ages.[8] With her easygoing style, however, she soon developed a reputation for not being able to control her students. After almost three years of teaching at Salem, she was asked to leave. She soon found another teaching position in nearby Methuen, Massachusetts.

In the fall of 1888, Rob and Jeanie were admitted to Lawrence High School, the same school their father had attended. They commuted from Salem to Lawrence by train each day, their grandfather providing the train fare. Many of the town kids from Lawrence looked down on kids from Salem as being country bumpkins. The Frost children were teased, and Rob, for his part, became determined to prove them wrong.[9]

As a freshman, Rob signed up for classes that would prepare him for college. His ninth-grade schedule included ancient Greek and Roman history, Greek and Latin, algebra, and geometry. By this time Rob was ready for the challenge. He made a strong start in all his classes, and by the end of the year he had the best grades in his class.

A more confident Rob began his sophomore year

at Lawrence.[10] Along with his studies, he joined the debating team. He also decided to try his hand at writing poetry. He drew his inspiration from *The History of the Conquest of Mexico,* a book by William Hickling Prescott about the conquest of the Aztec Indians in the sixteenth century by the Spanish conquistadores. Rob sympathized with the courage and dignity of the Aztecs in their efforts to defend their land and culture against their Spanish conquerors.[11]

By the end of the year Rob had the best grades in his class.

One day soon after finishing the book, Rob was walking to his grandmother's house after school. A poem about the Aztecs began to take shape in his mind. Aided by the steady rhythm of his footsteps and his books swinging from their book strap as he walked, he created verse after verse in his head. This poem, "La Noche Triste" ("The Sad Night"), was about the Spanish conquistadores' temporary retreat from the Aztec city of Tenochtitlan. Once he got to his grandmother's house, Rob sat down at the kitchen table and quickly jotted down his verses. Years later he would remember the event: "I had never written a poem before, and as I walked, it appeared like a revelation."[12]

The next day Rob left the poem on the desk of the chief editor of the Lawrence High School newspaper, the *Bulletin.* Even though he was just a sophomore, his poem was published on the first page of the *Bulletin* in April 1890.

Thrilled with his accomplishment, Rob set to work again. His next poem, "Song of the Wave," described what he remembered of the terrifying power of a storm over the ocean one night when he was a little boy in San Francisco. It was published the next month in the *Bulletin* and would become the kernel for another poem, "Once by the Pacific," which he would write years later.

During his sophomore year, Rob became friends with a senior named Carl Burrell. Almost ten years older than Rob, Carl had left high school before grad-

Jeanie Frost

uating but later returned to earn his diploma. One of Carl's interests was botany, or the study of plants. Over time Rob became interested in botany as well. In fact, it would be a lifelong passion for him and a major influence on his poetry.

Returning to Salem after a summer spent working in Maine, Rob was ready to begin his junior year at Lawrence. He faced a tough schedule of Latin and Greek, including Latin and Greek composition (writing). He also remained on the debating team. Despite the challenge, he was determined to maintain his place at the head of his class.

Also that year, Rob began to prepare for his college entrance examinations. He was hoping to be admitted to Harvard, in Cambridge, Massachusetts, where his father had studied. The exams would cover Greek and Latin, along with Greek and Roman history, algebra, geometry, and English literature. They lasted seven hours and required tremendous preparation in order to pass.

Rob began his senior year at Lawrence in an enviable position. He was at the top of his class academically, chief editor of the *Bulletin*, a respected debater, and popular with his classmates. He had also made the varsity football team. On top of all that, he had passed all his college entrance examinations.

While Rob's high school career was a complete success, his sister, Jeanie, had a far different experience. For several years she had suffered from insomnia—the inability to sleep—along with periods of deep depression, crying fits, and panic attacks. In the winter of her senior year, she developed typhoid fever, a potentially serious disease caused by typhoid bacteria, and had to drop out of high school altogether.

As Rob observed his sister's decline, he realized his own ability to fall prey to the downward spiral of depression. It was a demon he would battle for the rest of his life. For the time being, he dealt with the problem by keeping his life as busy as possible. He was afraid that if he ever gave in to the depression that seemed to hound him, his life would fall apart, just as Jeanie's had.[13]

As his senior year drew to a close, Rob had the highest grades in his class, although another student, Elinor Miriam White, was close on his heels. Elinor sat next to Rob in their homeroom class, and they chatted from time to time. Their paths also crossed sometimes in the school halls. During the winter of their senior year, the two struck up a friendship. They found they shared a love of poetry. Later that spring, Rob and Elinor became a couple.

By the end of their senior year, the high school principal had decided that Rob's and Elinor's grades were so close, they would share the title of valedictorian of the class of 1892. Rob was given the honor of being the last of thirteen speakers at the graduation ceremonies. He titled his speech "A Monument to After-Thought Unveiled." But the honor came with a price. The thought of speaking before an audience filled him with terror. As the graduation day approached, Rob adjusted the seating arrangement to make sure he was by the aisle in case he needed to make a quick exit to calm his nerves.

Finally, graduation day dawned. As the eleventh

☀PROGRAMME.☀

14. VOCAL SOLO.—"Good Bye, Sweet Day."   *Vannah*
        LILLIAN G. CATE.

15. ESSAY.—"Mary Lyon's Influence in the Education of Women."
        HATTIE W. CARTER.

16. CLASS HISTORY.
        AMY G. WILLAN.

17. CHORUS.—"Columbia's Jubilee."   *Trowbridge*

18. ESSAY, (of Valedictory Rank.)—"Conversation as a Force
    in Life."
        ELLINOR M. WHITE.

19. ORIGINAL DECLAMATION, with Valedictory Address.—
    "A Monument to Afterthought Unveiled,"
        ROBERT L. FROST.

20. AWARDING OF HOOD, VALPEY AND BULLETIN PRIZES
        BY SUPERINTENDENT W. C. BATES.

21. CLASS HYMN.
        WORDS BY ROBERT L. FROST.
        Music by Beethoven.

    There is a nook among the alders
    Still sleeping to the cat-bird's "Hush";
        Below, a long stone-bridge is bending
    Above a runnel's silent rush.

    A dreamer hither often wanders
    And gathers many a snow-white stone;
        He weighs them, poised upon his fingers,
    Divining each one's silvery tone.

    He drops them! When the stream makes music,
    Fair visions with its vault-voice swell:
        And so, for us, the future rises,
    As thought-stones stir our heart's "Farewell!"

Both Rob and Elinor, the two top students in the graduating class, spoke at the ceremony. Rob also wrote the words for the class hymn.

speaker was finishing, Rob quietly left the auditorium, shaking with fright and sick to his stomach. He found a sink and doused his face with cold water. Then he returned to the auditorium just in time for his place on the program. He was so nervous that he raced through his presentation, despite hours of preparation. Once he had finished his speech and could sit down, he was called onstage yet again to receive a medal of excellence for his four years of outstanding scholarship and citizenship.

With graduation over, the fall loomed, and Rob and Elinor would be heading in different directions to college. While Rob had first intended to go to Harvard, his grandmother frowned on the idea, thinking the school had a reputation for excessive drinking and partying.[14] When his math teacher suggested Dartmouth College, in Hanover, New Hampshire, as an alternative, the idea stuck. Elinor, on the other hand, was going to St. Lawrence University, in Canton, New York. To seal their commitment to each other while they were apart, the couple made a secret pact to marry. In addition, by this time Rob had made another monumental decision. He wanted to be a poet.[15]

4
DEAD ENDS

That last summer before he started college was a delightful one for Rob. He had an easy job at a mill in Lawrence and spent his evenings and weekends with Elinor. The couple often took walks together, sometimes taking Elinor's grandfather's rowboat out for a romantic ride on the Merrimac River.

Rob and Elinor were in love, and Rob wanted to get married immediately. Elinor, however, was more practical. Their lives were just getting started. She also knew that her parents had concerns about whether Rob was an ideal match for her.[1]

Rob reluctantly headed off to Hanover, New Hampshire, to begin his studies at Dartmouth. Because of his outstanding high school record, Dartmouth had offered him a scholarship that covered most of his

Rob and Elinor enjoyed
boating on the Merrimac
River.

tuition. Grandfather Frost agreed to help
by paying for his room and board.

Rob took three courses—Greek, Latin, and
advanced algebra. In addition, all students were
required to attend chapel early each morning and
church every Sunday. In his spare time, Rob enjoyed
hiking all over Hanover, often taking long walks along
the Connecticut River. He usually went alone, study-
ing nature and thinking about possible lines for
whatever poem he was working on at the time.

One day, while browsing in a bookstore, Rob came
across *A Golden Treasury*, by Francis Palgrave. First

published in 1861, the book is considered a comprehensive collection of British verse and poems for that time. It would become an important source for Rob as he began to analyze how some of the world's best poetry was written.

Rob made another significant discovery at the Dartmouth library: *The Independent*, a nationally sold and well-respected magazine devoted to publishing and reviewing the work of current poets. Up until then Rob had been unaware that such a magazine existed. He was thrilled to find it, because he knew it would be a valuable resource for keeping up with the world of poetry.[2] He also hoped that one day a poem of his might be published in the magazine.[3]

While he was at Hanover, Rob missed Elinor terribly and wrote her long letters. At the same time, he was frustrated because she seemed to be getting along very well at St. Lawrence without him.[4]

In addition to his loneliness, Rob soon found that life at Dartmouth did not suit him. By this time in his life, he resented being told what to read and study.[5] Instead, he wanted to follow his own interests, to be allowed to read and learn according to his own schedule. Reflecting on that time in his life, Frost later admitted, "I was getting

> **Rob hoped that one day a poem of his might be published in *The Independent*.**

Frost was not happy at Dartmouth College.

past the point where I could show any interest in any task not self-imposed."[6] He also thought his college courses were irrelevant to his life: "I couldn't make out what the thing I was doing in class and out had to do with what . . . I wanted to become."[7]

Before the end of his first semester, Rob walked away from Dartmouth. He left without notifying the school or saying good-bye to anyone, except for one friend, Preston Shirley.

As a star student of Lawrence High School, Rob had proven his intellectual ability and willingness to work hard. To turn down a college education was an unexpected move.[8] He felt some guilt about his decision to leave Dartmouth, later saying, "But that I should so treat a grandfather—one who had sincerely offered a college education to a promising valedictorian—put me out of all repute in Lawrence. A cloud of puzzlement hung over me as an obstinate, indecisive young fool."[9]

Rob knew his leaving Dartmouth would be a disappointment to his family and a shock to anyone who knew him, but he had an excuse ready. He said that he needed to go home to help his mother. She was in her third year of teaching in

Frost's Thoughts on Education

Frost's disdain for education that consisted of memorizing facts and quoting what others wrote lasted all his life. He later said, "The only education worth anything is self-education. All the rest consists of school work, textbooks, training, aids to help distinguish one fact from another without helping us to tell true values from false."[10]

Methuen and was once again having difficulty keeping her class of seventh-graders and eighth-graders under control.

Arriving home, Frost took over his mother's class. At that time, using physical force to discipline students was an accepted practice, so Frost came to his mother's class prepared. Using a cane on two of the biggest boys, he got the class under control in no time.

That spring Frost went to Salem, New Hampshire, where the White family had rented a house. They wanted to provide a change of scenery for Elinor's sister, Ada, who was suffering from severe anxiety attacks.

Elinor took a temporary leave of absence from school that spring so she could join her family in Salem as well. Seeing her, Rob found himself more in love than ever. Again he proposed an immediate marriage, but again Elinor said no. She was concerned because he had quit Dartmouth. She did not want to marry a man who had no steady job and could not support her financially.[11]

> **Seeing Elinor, Rob found himself more in love than ever. Again he proposed marriage, and again she said no.**

In the fall of 1893, Elinor returned to St. Lawrence to begin her sophomore year. Rob, with time on his hands, turned to writing poetry. He wrote the poem "Bereft" in August 1893. The poem expresses his feelings of loneliness, along with his sense of having no direction in his life.[12]

Bereft

Where had I heard this wind before
Change like this to a deeper roar?
What would it take my standing there for,
Holding open a restive door,
Looking down hill to a frothy shore?
Summer was past and day was past.
Somber clouds in the west were massed.
Out in the porch's sagging floor,
Leaves got up in a coil and hissed,
Blindly struck at my knee and missed.
Something sinister in the tone
Told me my secret must be known:
Word I was in the house alone
Somehow must have gotten abroad,
Word I was in my life alone,
Word I had no one left but God.

With Elinor back at St. Lawrence, Frost got a job at the Arlington Woolen Mill in Lawrence. He was hired to keep the lights going in the machine room. It was a boring job, and Frost was embarrassed to be working in a job that did not challenge him.[13] Yet he had no plan for the direction his life should take.

On sunny days the lights at the mill were not used and Frost had time to himself. At those times, he hid from his supervisor on the roof of the building. He did not want to be caught with nothing to do and be given extra work. Alone in his hiding place, he read and studied the works of William Shakespeare. He analyzed how Shakespeare balanced the rhythm of his poetry against the natural patterns of speech.[14] At night Frost continued to work on his own poetry.

In addition to being embarrassed about working at the mill, Frost was often late for work. He liked to sleep late in the mornings, a habit that would continue throughout his life. Every morning, the mill sounded a loud whistle signaling that employees should be in their places ready for work. Those not making it through the mill gates by the time the whistle blew had to stand outside for a while before they were let in. In addition, their pay for that day was cut.

One day in February 1894, Frost ran up to the gate, only to hear the mill whistle blowing. He was late again. By that time, he had had enough of mill work. He was humiliated and discouraged by the dead ends he had chosen so far in his life.[15] So, just as he had done at Dartmouth, he simply walked away from the mill gates that day and did not return.

5

A SLOW START

Robert Frost was floundering. He knew he wanted to be a poet, but how should he get started? And how could he possibly support a family in that line of work? It seemed that being a poet would mean a life of poverty.[1] Still, he was not ready to give up.

In the fall of 1893, Frost composed what he later considered to be his first true poem.[2] He called it "My Butterfly: An Elegy." An elegy is a sad or mournful poem. He later described writing the poem, saying, "I wrote it all in one go in the kitchen of our house in Tremont Street. I locked the door and all the time I was working, Jeanie my sister tried to batter it down and get in."[3]

The idea for the poem was sparked by a fragile butterfly wing he found among some dead leaves at

Dartmouth. Beautiful and delicate, the wing fascinated him. It seemed to be a symbol of the fragility of life.[4]

With "My Butterfly," Frost realized that he wanted to write poetry that used ordinary speech.[5] He still included some formal words such as "thy," "thee," and "oft " in the poem. Yet as he continued to develop his style, he would drop that kind of language altogether, replacing it with ordinary words used by ordinary people.[6] Thinking back on "My Butterfly" later, Frost said, "The first stanza—well, that's nothing. But the second—it's as good as anything I've ever written. It was the beginning of me."[7]

> My Butterfly (second stanza)
> *The gray grass is scarce dappled with the snow;*
> *Its two banks have not shut upon the river;*
> *But it is long ago—*
> *It seems forever—*
> *Since first I saw thee glance,*
> *With all the dazzling other ones,*
> *In airy dalliance,*
> *Precipitate in love,*
> *Tossed, tangled, whirled and whirled above,*
> *Like a limp rose-wreath in a fairy dance.*

Frost sent his poem to *The Independent* with the hope that it be selected for the magazine. To his delight, the editors quickly responded that they liked the poem and wanted to publish it. Sending his thanks for their acceptance of his poem, Frost wrote, "The memory of your note will be a fresh pleasure to me when I awaken for a good many mornings to come. . . . As for submitting more of my work, you may imagine I shall be only too glad to avail myself of your kindly interest."[8]

He received $15 from the magazine as payment for their right to publish it. The magazine's editor, Dr. William Hayes Ward, and his sister, Susan, would become friends of Frost's over the years, offering him advice and encouragement with his work. With high hopes for a career as a poet, Frost later wrote to Susan Ward, "It is only a matter of time now when I shall throw off the mask and declare for literateur mean it poverty or riches."[9]

To help Frost, Dr. Ward contacted a friend in Lawrence, the Reverend W. A. Wolcott, asking him to visit Frost and give him advice. Wolcott praised the poem but said he did not consider it to be true poetry. The words Frost used in the poem were not poetic. For the most part they were words people would use when naturally

A Generous Offer

Grandfather Frost had a proposal for his grandson. He offered to pay Rob's living expenses for a year while he tried to make a living as a poet. In exchange, Rob had to agree that if he was still not supporting himself by the end of the year, he would abandon his dream and get a regular job. Despite his grandfather's sincerity and generosity, Rob turned the offer down. He knew that it would take far more than a year to become a successful poet.[10]

talking. Frost agreed, saying that had been his purpose.[11]

Having left the woolen mill, Frost needed to find another job quickly. His mother had recently lost her job at Methuen, so money was especially scarce. Frost went to see the head of the school board in Salem, New Hampshire, about a job and was hired to teach children ages six through twelve. He found that he enjoyed working with children.[12] Still, his dream of writing poetry for a living nagged at the back of his mind.[13]

With a steady and respectable job as a teacher in Salem, Frost had one of his problems solved, at least for the time being. But his other problem remained. He worried that Elinor did not love him anymore.[14] She seemed to be having a wonderful time at college without him, and he was afraid that she had fallen in love with someone else.[15]

> **His dream of writing poetry for a living nagged at the back of his mind.**

The summer of 1894, Frost again tried to persuade Elinor to marry him. She told him she would do so after she graduated, but only if he were able to support the two of them. She also agreed to take extra courses the next year so she could graduate early.

That fall Elinor returned to school. As a gift to her, Frost compiled five of his poems, including "My

Knowing that Elinor was not ready to make a serious commitment left Frost feeling miserable and alone.

Butterfly." He had them professionally printed on high-quality paper and bound with the title *Twilight* in gold letters on the cover. He ordered only two copies of the book: one for Elinor and one for himself. With this gift, he hoped to convince her that he had promise as a poet.[16] After buying a new suit for the occasion, he took an overnight train to Canton, New York, to deliver his gift in person.

Unfortunately, Frost's plans did not work out as he had hoped. Elinor was surprised and rather irritated to see him on her doorstep. For his part, Frost had no idea that women students were allowed to entertain gentlemen visitors only at certain times during the day. Elinor accepted the book without comment, told him to return to Lawrence on the first available train, and closed the door.[17]

Devastated by her cool response, Frost tore up his copy of his book and caught the next train home.

Beside himself with grief and anger, and terrified that
he had lost Elinor forever, Frost abruptly left home in
early November, leaving no note as to where he was
going. He traveled by train and steamship from
Lawrence to Norfolk, Virginia. Then he went on foot
to a place called Dismal Swamp, located some twenty
miles along the Virginia–North Carolina border.

In Dismal Swamp, Frost found the perfect environment to suit his mood. It was dark and gloomy, an
overgrown wilderness. He was not sure what to do
once he got there, although he had vague and romantic thoughts of dying there, in the hope that he would
make Elinor suffer.[18]

While wandering around in the middle of the
night in Dismal Swamp with no plan for what to do
next, he happened upon a group of duck hunters. He
accepted their offer of a ride to Elizabeth City, North
Carolina, where he stowed away on a freight train that
took him to Washington, D.C. Once there, with no
money, he persuaded a policeman to let him spend the
night in jail so he could get rest, food, and shelter. His
next stop was Baltimore, where he got a job delivering
groceries. Finally realizing that his show of running
from his problems was useless, he sent a telegram to his
mother asking her to send him money so he could buy
a train ticket home. He was home by the end of
November, three weeks after his abrupt departure.

By that time, Frost had decided that the best way

Frost tried a few different jobs in his quest to figure out how to earn a living.

to get Elinor back was to get a job. Thinking that journalism might be a good fit for his skills and interests, he took a position as a reporter with the Lawrence *Daily American*. As a reporter, he was expected to pry into people's private affairs, but that made him uncomfortable.[19] He quit the *Daily American* after just two weeks.

His next job, as a writer at the *Sentinel*, did not last much longer. He did not like working under the pressure of a deadline. For Frost, deadlines took all the fun and creativity out of writing. He was also afraid that news writing would ruin his progress as a poet.[20]

In mid-March 1895, Elinor returned home from school. Frost met her at her home, but again things did not go well. They had a big fight, which resulted in his taking back his engagement ring and throwing it into the coal stove in her kitchen. Then he left for Boston to visit a friend and cool down. By the time he returned to Lawrence, Elinor had sent him a letter of apology. The two patched up their differences and got back on steady footing.

In the meantime, Frost's mother had decided to start a private school of her own in Lawrence. It opened in the fall of 1895 with twenty students. By then Elinor had graduated from college, and Mrs. Frost wanted to hire her as a French teacher. With Rob once again teaching in Salem, their futures looked fairly stable, and so Elinor agreed to marry Rob.

Elinor's father still opposed the match. He saw his potential son-in-law as lazy and undependable in terms of keeping a job.[21] Even so, Elinor stuck to her decision. The couple married on December 19, 1895. Elinor's father did not attend the wedding.

As 1896 dawned, one dream of Rob Frost's had come true. His love for Elinor had given him the determination to fight for her despite all odds. At last, she was his wife. Fulfilling his dream of making a living as a poet would not come as quickly or as easily.

6
DIFFICULT
CIRCUMSTANCES

Frost was not making enough money from teaching to rent or buy a house. So he and Elinor moved in with Belle and Jeanie, starting their married life together in Lawrence. By March, Elinor was expecting their first baby. Elliott was born on September 25, 1896.

The following summer, Frost decided he needed to go back to college. With his prospects of earning a living as a poet looking impractical, he thought he might like to teach Latin or Greek at the high school level.[1] To do that, however, he would need a college degree.

Frost wrote to the Dean of Students at Harvard University, in Cambridge, Massachusetts, requesting admittance to the university. He was accepted and began his studies there as a freshman in the fall of 1897. Grandfather Frost paid his expenses.

Deciding that he should earn a college degree, Frost enrolled at Harvard University.

Despite his overall success at Harvard, Frost's time there was cut short. In the spring of his sophomore year, he began suffering from nervous anxiety and depression, which led to severe chest and stomach pains. He was concerned that he might be getting tuberculosis, the disease that had killed his father.[2] Too ill to continue with his studies, he quit the program at Harvard in the spring of 1899 and returned to his family in Lawrence.

Once back at home with Elinor and Elliott, along with their new baby, Lesley, who was born in April, Frost felt sure that his health would improve.[3] He was wrong; his condition only worsened. His doctor suggested that he take up farming as a way to get more fresh air and exercise. The doctor thought outdoor work might lift Frost's spirits and rid him of his physical ailments. He and Elinor decided to find a nearby farm where they could raise chickens.

In June 1899, the little family moved to Methuen, Massachusetts, to start a chicken farm. They rented a property with the help of a loan from Frost's grandfather. Knowing nothing about raising chickens, Frost got advice and help from a local veterinarian. He bought enough eggs to get started and was hopeful that his health would improve with this plan. Over the next year, Frost set about building pens for his chickens, along with shelters for the incubators where their eggs would hatch. To his relief, he started feeling better and found that he enjoyed the work.[5]

That fall, Frost's mother was diagnosed

Studying at Harvard

Frost's courses at Harvard included Greek, Latin, philosophy, and English. With his vast knowledge of literature and writing, he was humiliated at having to take a first-year English class.[4] To add insult to injury, some of the poems he submitted in class were not well received by his English professor.

Discouraged and frustrated, he did not apply himself in that class, and his grades reflected his lack of effort. On the other hand, Frost did very well with his other classes and received an award for his outstanding work in them.

with cancer and given less than a year to live. She moved in with her son and his family, so they could take care of her.

Early in the summer of 1900, the Frosts' son, Elliott, now almost four, suddenly became ill with a high fever and severe stomach cramps. Frost had his mother's doctor examine Elliott. The doctor left some pills for the child, but they had no effect. The Frosts got another doctor to see their son, but Elliott could not be saved. He died of cholera on July 8, 1900.

The Frosts were utterly devastated by Elliott's death. Elinor fell into a deep depression, becoming very quiet and refusing to talk about her feelings. Frost felt responsible because he had not gotten the help his son needed sooner.[6] To him, it was as if he had murdered his own child.[7]

Two of Frost's best poems, which he would write years later, are about the death of a child. "Home Burial" expresses how he dealt with his grief by talking about his feelings, while his wife bottled hers up with silence. The poem conveys the miscommunication that can happen between men and women.[8] Another poem, "'Out, Out, ___,'" is about working through grief by getting on with life.[9]

In August the Frosts were forced to move Belle into a nearby sanitarium, as her condition was declining quickly and she needed more medical care than the

Frosts could provide at home. She would die there three months later.

On top of their grief over their son's death and Belle's condition, the Frosts were also having financial difficulties. The farm was not bringing in enough money to cover their rent, and by September 1900 they were several months

Two of Frost's best poems are about the death of a child.

behind. When the landlady came to collect the rent, she was shocked by the condition of the house. Elinor's housekeeping skills were rather lax. The landlady found that chickens were running loose, dirty dishes were piled high in the sink, and dust and dirt were everywhere. With the house in such a state, and the Frost's inability to pay their rent, she told them they had to find another place to live.

Fortunately, Elinor's mother heard of a thirty-acre farm for sale near the village of Derry, New Hampshire. Just twelve miles from Lawrence, it had a farmhouse, a barn, a big vegetable garden, and an apple orchard. The property was in rather poor condition; at a minimum the house and barn both needed painting and new roofs. But the farm was priced reasonably.

Elinor was convinced this would be a good move for her family. So she gathered her courage and asked Grandfather Frost for yet another loan so they could buy the farm. He agreed to buy it himself and let his grandson rent it from him.

The house on the Derry farm was a small, rather plain two-story white frame structure with green shutters. It had no indoor plumbing; water was available from a pump outside the house. A stream ran through the south side of the property, and raspberries and blackberries grew wild throughout. With fields, pastureland, and several wooded acres, the farm appeared to be a good place for the Frosts and their children. The surrounding New Hampshire country-side was beautiful as well, with gently rolling hills and winding valleys.

At this point, Robert Frost was discouraged and depressed about the seemingly pointless directions he had taken in his life. Remembering that time, he later said, "The total failure of everything was on my mind, my conscience."[10] Yet the move to the Derry farm would lay the foundation for much of his poetry. Frost later reflected, "There was something about the experience at Derry which stayed in my mind, and was tapped for poetry in the years that came after."[11]

The Frosts moved in October 1900, and would live there for ten years. Much of Frost's best work would be written there. The setting was a good one for him to relax and feel close to nature, allowing the images that surrounded him to simmer in his mind. Eventually, he would translate them into poetry. He later referred to the years at Derry as, "a time when my eyes and ears were open, very open."[12]

Much of Frost's best work would be written at the Derry farm.

On the other hand, as Frost later said, "What I faced, [upon moving to the Derry property] I hadn't the slightest notion."[13] It would take six years to develop the farm and its products, including hay, eggs, and apples, and learn all the skills necessary to make it even moderately productive.

Frost also found that his approach to the routine of farm life differed from that of the other farmers in the area. They all rose very early in the morning, tended to their crops and livestock all day, and retired in the late afternoon. But Frost was on a different clock. It was unusual for him to begin work before noon. His neighbors shook their heads in disapproval at what they saw as his laziness.[14] As Frost later described it, "They [the farmers] would talk among themselves about my lack of energy. When they saw me sleeping away the better part of the day—well, it was quite too much for them. I was a failure in their eyes from the start. . . ."[15] But Frost was using his late-night hours, when the house was quiet and his family was asleep, to write.

Grandfather Frost died unexpectedly in the summer of 1901. He never saw his grandson succeed at his long-cherished dream of making a living as a poet. But he left him $500 annual allowance for ten years, which would increase to $800 each year after that. His will also stated that the Derry farm would become Frost's in 1911. In the meantime, Frost was relieved of paying rent. In addition, all other debts to his grandfather were forgiven.

As the years passed, the Frost family continued to grow. A son, Carol, was born in May 1902, and a daughter, Irma, in June 1903. Marjorie was born in March 1905. Isolated from other farms, the Frost children grew up playing together without the friendship of other children. They were also home-schooled. Elinor taught her children reading, handwriting, geography, and spelling. In addition, they were expected to memorize and recite a wide variety of poetry.

Frost taught the children two of his favorite subjects—botany and astronomy. To do that, he took them for long walks throughout their property. Frost called his walks "botanizing." With their father's guidance, the children learned the names of all the plants and animals they saw on their hikes. In winter he taught them to identify animal tracks they found in the snow. They also learned to recognize constellations in the night sky. Frost's daughter Lesley later wrote, "I learned, when I was very young, that flower and star, bird and fruit and running water, tree and doe and sunset, are wonderful facts of life."[16] Frost also

For the Frost children, the Derry farm was the place for playtime and schooltime, too.

encouraged his children's athletic development.[17] All became hearty walkers and expert tree climbers.

Money continued to be in short supply for the Frosts during their years in Derry. They got most of their food from the farm, but when other things were needed, they often had to buy them on credit. To complicate things, the family was often sick, requiring a doctor's attention, which further depleted their earnings.[18] At Christmas, with no extra money for gifts, the family made presents for each other.

With a growing family and never enough money, Frost knew he needed to find more income. He again turned to teaching, later reflecting, "It has always seemed strange to me that it was my children . . . who forced me out into the world and made me try and do something. You see, they got me into debt, and I had to find a way to pay out."[19]

Knowing he was looking for a teaching job, a friend put him in touch with the Reverend Charles Merriam in Derry. He was a member of the school board for Derry's Pinkerton Academy. When Frost met with Merriam about the possibility of a teaching job, he mentioned his poetry as a way to show his qualifications to teach. Merriam was impressed, and suggested that he read some of his work at an upcoming meeting of the Derry Men's League. It would be their spring banquet, and several Pinkerton teachers would be there.

Frost agreed, choosing to read his poem, "The Tuft of Flowers." He had written it ten years earlier after walking in a freshly mowed hay field one day. There, he came upon a little group of flowers that had not been cut down. He was touched by the sight of the fragile flowers that had survived, while cut hay lay all around them.

When the evening came for the Derry Men's League meeting, Frost was beside himself with nervousness. He was still terrified of speaking in public.[20] So when he was introduced, he asked Merriam to read the poem for him.

The Pinkerton Annual -- 1917

OUR ALMA MATER

After some Pinkerton Academy teachers heard Frost's poetry, they encouraged him to apply for a teaching job.

To his delight, the reading was a big success. Impressed with his work, the Pinkerton teachers in the audience thought Frost would make an excellent English teacher at the academy, and they urged him to apply.

Frost did not want to work full-time, so he agreed to teach two classes of sophomore English. He began in March 1906. Looking back, Frost credited his poem with moving his career forward. "Got me my first real job," he said. "I have never earned a cent except by and through verse. . . . Whole family owe their life to this poem. . . . ["The Tuft of Flowers."][21]

Pinkerton Academy was two miles from the Frost's farm, and Frost walked there each day, regardless of the weather. From the beginning, some of the other teachers viewed him with suspicion and jealousy.[22] For one thing, they thought he dressed too casually for a teacher. He never wore a tie, and kept the top button of his shirts informally unbuttoned. He also skipped the mandatory chapel services held at the school each morning. On top of that, he had no college degree.

Frost also used unconventional teaching methods, just as his mother had. Slumped far down in the chair at his desk, he sometimes read to his students. Other times they had discussions. As with his children, Frost required his students to memorize and recite various poems from Palgrave's *Golden Treasury*. And rather than assigning essay topics, he encouraged his students

Frost's unusual teaching style made him a favorite with students at Pinkerton Academy.

to write about their personal experiences and observations. He told them to take common experiences and write about them in uncommon ways.[23]

Frost soon became a very popular teacher with his students.[24] One student, John Bartlett, described Frost's way with them: "He seemed to have several times the interest in me that other teachers had."[25] Over time, Frost's teaching practices were noticed by Henry Clinton Morrison, the state superintendent of public instruction, who would later refer to him as the "best teacher in New Hampshire."[26]

The next year Frost taught English full-time at Pinkerton. He would continue on at the academy for a few years. In addition to his teaching duties, he coached the school's debating team and directed school plays, which were highly acclaimed in the community. He also became the adviser for the school's newspaper, *The Pinkerton Critic*.

Despite Frost's success as a teacher, his family once again experienced tragedy in June 1907. Their last child, named Elinor Bettina, died the day after she was born. Once again Frost and his wife had to deal with the loss of a child.

Because of his successful teaching methods, Frost was asked in 1909 to give a presentation to a group of New Hampshire teachers. Still very nervous about speaking in public, he tried to distract himself by putting a pebble in each of his shoes and walking around for a while before he spoke. His technique did not work; his stage fright remained. Despite his nervousness, the presentation was well received and led to others.

Frost always looked back at his years at the Derry farm as being critical for his development as a poet. "The only thing we had plenty of [at the farm] was time and seclusion. I couldn't have figured on what this life would give me in advance but it was right as a doctor's prescription."[27]

Frost left Pinkerton when the school term was over in 1911. He was exhausted from juggling his time between teaching, farming, and writing. The principal at Pinkerton, Ernest Silver, left the school in 1911 as well. He had accepted a job as principal of the New Hampshire State Normal School in Plymouth. It was a school that trained women to be teachers. Silver had enjoyed working with Frost at Pinkerton, and persuaded him to teach psychology and the history of education at the normal school. Frost agreed to a one-year commitment.

All during his years at the Derry farm, Frost had continued to work on his poetry, occasionally sending poems to various magazines. With the exception of several that were published periodically in *The Independent*, all others were rejected and returned to him. Frost's father had died at the age of thirty-four. Knowing his own health was not strong, Frost decided it was time to turn his full attention to writing before it was too late.

> **Frost was exhausted from juggling his time between teaching, farming, and writing.**

He and Elinor thought he needed a complete change of location in order to devote himself to his writing. The question was, where to go? They debated the advantages of Vancouver, British Columbia, and England. Finally, the time came to make the decision. Elinor tossed a coin, and England won. It would turn out to be critical to Frost's emerging career as a poet.

7

TURNING POINT

Within two weeks of their decision to go to England, the Frosts were aboard the SS *Parisian* and on their way. With money from the sale of the Derry farm, along with Grandfather Frost's annual allowance, Frost thought his family could survive financially for two or three years if they were very careful with their money.

They soon found a cottage to rent in Beaconsfield, about twenty miles north of London. The home had five bedrooms, along with a garden with fruit trees and a strawberry patch. It was called The Bungalow.

The Frosts quickly installed the few household items they had brought with them, including some rugs, a typewriter, and Elinor's rocking chair. Most important, they had brought Frost's Morris chair, from which he

Frost's favorite place to write was at his Morris chair with a board across the arms.

wrote by placing a board across the chair arms. "The chair I could write in had to have just the right arms to support a shelf stolen from the closet and not to interfere with my elbows," he later wrote.[1]

Soon after settling into their home, Frost sat down on the living room floor late one evening in front of the fire and pulled out the folders of poems he had been working on and saving over the past twenty years. Those he was dissatisfied with he tossed into the fire. Then he chose thirty-two poems from those that remained. They would become the contents of his first book, *A Boy's Will.*

The general theme of the poems Frost chose reflect the struggles that followed his days as a Dartmouth student. Since then, he had been trying to find the right direction for his life. The poems in *A Boy's Will* traced that journey.

In late October, Frost took his group of poems to a publishing house in London—David Nutt and Company, a small but respected firm that published poetry. Frost met with Mrs. Nutt, who was managing the firm at the time. She accepted Frost's manuscript for review. Just three days later he received a note from her saying that she would like to publish his poems.

Frost was ecstatic. He wrote, "I . . . have seldom been prouder of anything. You see, I had turned the trick, done it. I had found myself a publisher."[2]

The next month, Frost saw a notice in the November issue of *Poetry Review* magazine announcing the opening of a new book store in London which would devote its inventory to books of, or about, poetry. As part of the opening festivities, the store's manager was hosting an open house and poetry discussion on January 8. Poets and people interested in poetry were urged to come. Frost quickly decided to attend.

When he got to the bookshop that evening, it was so crowded that the only seat he could find was on the staircase. One of the people he met that night was poet Frank S. Flint. The two men struck up a conversation, and Flint, upon finding out that Frost was an American poet, asked if he had met Ezra Pound. A poet of note, with a reputation as a leading literary figure in England and the United States, Pound was also an American. Flint soon told Pound about Frost, and Pound sent a note to Frost inviting him to come for a visit.

After a couple of months, Frost happened to be in the area of Pound's home in London, and decided to stop in to introduce himself. He told Pound of his book, *A Boy's Will,* which was nearing publication. Pound, eager to assess Frost's work, suggested they both walk to the publisher's offices right then to get an advance copy.

Once back at his home with Frost's book, Pound read through some of the poems while Frost waited. Then he suggested rather abruptly that Frost leave; he wanted to submit a review of the book.

This was a stroke of great luck for Frost. A review of his book by Ezra Pound would be widely read by literary people—the kind of people who bought poetry books. A positive review would help boost the book's sales.

Published in April 1913, *A Boy's Will* received many positive reviews. Pound's review appeared in *Poetry* magazine. While he pointed out what he considered to be some weaknesses in Frost's work, he also wrote that the book "has the tang of the New

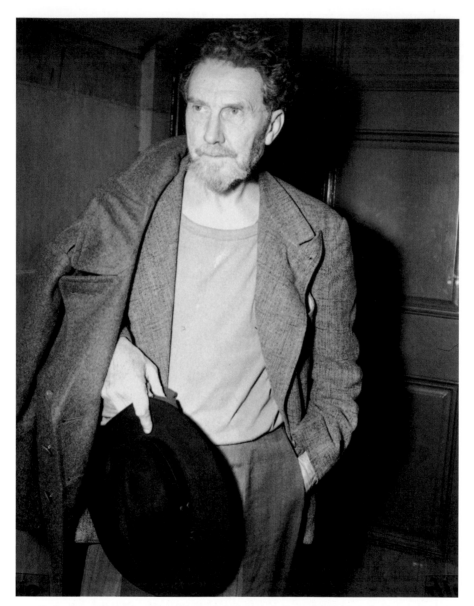

Being praised by the important poet Ezra Pound, above, gave a boost to Frost's career as a poet.

Hampshire woods. . . . This man has the good sense to speak naturally and to paint the thing, the thing as he sees it. . . ."[3] Another very positive review ended, "We have not the slightest idea who Mr. Robert Frost may be, but we welcome him unhesitatingly to the ranks of poets born. . . ."[4]

All during his time in England, Frost made every effort to get to know poets and writers there. Along with Frank Flint, he became friends with a number of people in London's literary circles. One in particular was Edward Thomas. They were introduced in February 1913, and Thomas would become one of Frost's closest friends.

Thomas, his wife, and three children lived southwest of London. Thomas wrote travel books, biographies, essays, and reviews. As their relationship developed, Frost encouraged Thomas to write poetry as well. Frost later described their friendship by saying, "Thomas and I had become so inseparable that we came to be looked on as some sort of literary Siamese twins . . . with a spiritual bond holding us together."[5]

With the success of *A Boy's Will* still fresh in his mind, Frost soon began pulling together a new set of poems for his second book, *North of Boston*. It would include only sixteen poems, but several, such as "Mending Wall," "Home Burial," and "After Apple-Picking," are considered some of his best work.

In April 1914, the Frosts moved from Beaconsfield

to a house near Dymock, England. It was a rural area, and most of the local people were farmers or herders. The Frosts moved at the encouragement of another poet and friend, Lascelles Abercrombie, who lived near Dymock. Another poet, Wilfred Gibson, lived in the area as well.

The Frosts rented a 350-year-old cottage there, called Little Iddens. It was a very small house, with only two bedrooms and another little nook that could be used as a sleeping area. The floors on the first story were of brick, worn smooth after so many years. The ceilings were low and the windows tiny. The Frosts fell in love with the house because of its age and charm. With its vegetable garden and lovely views, Little Iddens reminded them a lot of the farm in Derry.[8]

North of Boston was released in May 1914. It was very well received by critics. Edward Thomas reviewed *North of Boston* in the *Daily News*, writing, "These poems are revolutionary because they lack the exaggeration of rhetoric. . . . Their language is free from the poetical words and forms that are the chief material of secondary poets. . . ."[9]

The Sound of Sense

Over the years Frost had been formulating a theory to describe the kind of poetry he was writing. He called it "the sound of sense." He thought that the rhythms and sounds of words when read should convey meaning, as well as the words themselves.[6] After hearing the conversational speech of the local New Hampshire farmers, he knew that theirs was the sound he was looking to create in his work. "I was after poetry that talked," he later told a friend.[7]

Wilfred Gibson also reviewed the book, writing, "Mr. Frost has turned the living speech of men and women into poetry."[10] In recognition of his "sound of sense" theory, another reviewer wrote, "[Frost] seems to be trying to capture and hold within metrical patterns the very tones of speech—the rise and fall, the stressed pauses and little hurries, of spoken language."[11]

That summer, Frost's closest friend, Edward Thomas, and his family joined the group of poets living in and around Dymock. Together they enjoyed the summer months, taking countless "botanizing" walks and talking about poetry, politics, and philosophy.

Thomas's wife, Helen, recorded her observations of their friendship: "They were always together and when not exploring the country they sat in the shade of a tree smoking and talking endlessly of literature and poetry in particular."[12] She further wrote of the easy friendship among the poets and their families: "When it was wet we all assembled in the Frost's cottage; and as there were only two chairs in the living room we sat on the floor with our backs against the wall, talking or singing folk songs in which of course the children joined."[13] "1914 was our year," Frost later wrote, "I never had, I never shall have another such year of friendship."[14]

"Mr. Frost has turned the living speech of men and women into poetry."

While in England, the Frost family rented a cottage they called Little Iddens.

In June 1914, political tensions erupted in Europe, with Germany declaring war on Russia and France. When the Germans invaded Belgium in August, Great Britain declared war on Germany. World War I had begun. Shortly thereafter, Frost's friend Edward Thomas enlisted in the army to fight for Great Britain.

In September, the Frosts moved from Little Iddens to the Abercrombies' house, called The Gallows. With the two families living in one house, they could reduce their living expenses. By this time Frost was very low on funds, and with the war, book publishing had come to a halt in England.

While living at the Gallows, Frost began writing one of his most enduring poems, "The Road Not Taken." He later said he wrote it with his friend

Edward Thomas in mind; yet many would view the poem as reflecting Frost's own life journey.

The Road Not Taken

Two roads diverged in a yellow wood,
And sorry I could not travel both
And be one traveler, long I stood
And looked down one as far as I could
To where it bent in the undergrowth;

Then took the other, as just as fair,
And having perhaps the better claim,
Because it was grassy and wanted wear;
Though as for that, the passing there
Had worn them really about the same,

And both that morning equally lay
In leaves no step had trodden black.
Oh, I kept the first for another day!
Yet knowing how way leads on to way,
I doubted if I should ever come back.

I shall be telling this with a sigh
Somewhere ages and ages hence:
Two roads diverged in a wood, and I—
I took the one less traveled by,
And that has made all the difference.

By December 1914, Frost was ready to return home. For one thing, he had run out of money. At the same time, Frost also learned from Mrs. Nutt that Henry Holt and Company was selling his books in the United States. Now he had a publisher at home.[15] In addition, Germany was threatening to blockade British ports. If that happened before the Frosts left, they might be unable to get back home until the war was over.

So the Frosts returned to the United States in February 1915, on the American ship, the SS *St. Paul.* Before leaving England, Frost wrote a letter to Frank S. Flint, the poet he had met at Henry Munro's Poetry Bookshop more than two years earlier. He wanted to thank him for introducing him to Ezra Pound. Frost wrote, ". . . I must at least say goodbye to the man who opened England to me."[16]

8

MOVING FORWARD

Frost had mixed feelings about returning to the United States. Although he had missed his native land, he was worried that he might be a failure as a poet in America.[1] He was also discouraged. Despite the success of his books in England, Mrs. Nutt had paid him no royalties for their sales. He was beginning to resign himself to the fact that he could not support himself and his family as a poet.[2] He arrived in New York tired and uncertain of his future.

Frost used the last of his money to buy train tickets for his family to return to New Hampshire. They would stay with the Lynch family in the village of Bethlehem, high up in the White Mountains. The Lynches and Frosts were longtime friends. The Frosts had spent several summers with them, renting rooms in their home so that Frost could escape the pollen that caused his severe hay fever every summer. This time, the Frosts planned to stay until they found a farm to buy.

As they made their way to catch their train, Frost happened to stop by a newsstand where a copy of a new magazine, *The New Republic*, was displayed. The magazine's cover announced that the issue included book reviews by renowned American poet Amy Lowell. Interested, Frost used one of his last few coins to buy a copy. Later he said, ". . . that fifty cents was destined to buy me more satisfaction than any other half-dollar I had ever broke to spend."[3]

Inside the magazine Frost was astonished to find a prominent review by Lowell of *North of Boston*. She called it "a book of unusual power and sincerity."[4] Frost later wrote, "When I saw her review it seemed to me that America was holding out friendly hands to welcome me."[5] Just as with Ezra Pound's review of *A Boy's Will* in *Poetry* magazine two years earlier, this was an important review in an important magazine. Frost knew it would get attention.

He sent his family on to New Hampshire without him, and hurried to the offices of his American publisher, Henry Holt and Company. Once there, he was able to meet with Alfred Harcourt, the head of the trade book department. Harcourt told him the happy news that he already had a royalty check from *The New Republic* in payment for their publishing his poem

This family picture of Elinor and Robert Frost with their children was taken in 1915: front, Marjorie and Carol; back, Lesley and Irma.

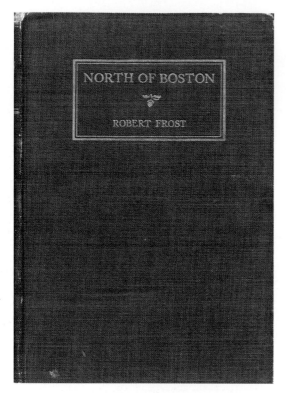

Other American poets praised Frost's *North of Boston*. Its success made him one of the most popular poets in the country.

"The Death of the Hired Man." Harcourt also said that *North of Boston* was selling well. Frost stayed in New York for several days, using his time to promote himself and his work by meeting with various literary figures, members of the Poetry Society of America, and editors of *The New Republic.*

From New York, Robert Frost headed to South Fork, Pennsylvania, to visit his sister, Jeanie, who was teaching there. Still suffering from ongoing nervous anxiety, she was finding it difficult to hold on to a job for more than a year. Although he and his sister had never gotten along very well, this was a relatively pleasant visit. Frost listened patiently to his sister's complaints and fears, and he tried to give her advice and guidance.

Once Frost joined his family in New Hampshire, they began looking for a farm to buy. They soon found one about two miles from the town of Franconia. The house was small and had no bathroom or furnace.

But the Frosts were used to living with inconveniences. And the farm was surrounded by mountains, with breathtaking views from every direction. So they proceeded to buy the property.

Just before moving to the farm in Franconia, Frost began receiving invitations to lecture and to read his poetry. The Phi Beta Kappa Society, an honor society at Tufts College near Boston, asked him to read some of his poems at their annual meeting in May. The Boston Authors' Club also wanted him to speak at one of their luncheons.

Despite his fear of speaking in public, Frost was delighted with the opportunities.[6] In just a matter of months after arriving in the United States, he was beginning to be recognized for his work. In addition, he was paid a fee for each of his speaking engagements, which gave a boost to his always-meager finances.

At Tufts, Frost read three as yet unpublished

A Way to Connect

Rather than project the image of a sophisticated intellectual, Frost chose to accentuate the low-key side of his personality. He wanted people to see him as a rustic, unambitious poet-farmer. He spoke in an easygoing, unpretentious way, using folksy humor and anecdotes throughout his talks. He also used uncomplicated, straightforward words that underscored his image as a man of the land. With his hair tousled, he usually wore the casual, wrinkled clothes he wore at home, including heavy farmer's boots.[7] Just as with his poems, Frost wanted to connect not only with intellectuals, but with ordinary people.

poems. He chose them well; they would become three of his best-known and beloved poems: "The Road Not Taken," "Birches," and "The Sound of Trees."

While in Boston, Frost met the poet and critic Louis Untermeyer. He had given *North of Boston* a favorable review in an April edition of the *Chicago Evening Post*. Over time, the two men would become close friends.

Frost also visited Ellery Sedgwick, the editor of *The Atlantic Monthly* magazine. He had sent many poems to *The Atlantic Monthly* over the years, and all had been rejected. He hoped that with Amy Lowell's review of *North of Boston*, he would be able to sell Sedgwick some poems for the magazine. The two men had a cordial meeting. Sedgwick was definitely interested in developing a business relationship with Frost. By the time their meeting was over, Frost had sold Sedgwick the rights to print three of his poems in *The Atlantic Monthly*.

Throughout his career, Frost actively pursued poets, critics, editors, and other contacts who could help promote his books. He knew that being aggressive was necessary to succeed.[8] His ambition propelled him past any fears or insecurity he might have in introducing his work to others who might help it get exposure.

Meanwhile, sales of *North of Boston* continued steadily. Holt had begun with 150 copies they had

Frost and his son, Carol.

purchased from Mrs. Nutt in England, but those were quickly sold. So they ordered a reprinting of thirteen hundred more. With that book's success, Holt also released *A Boy's Will* in May.

After his speaking engagement at Tufts, Frost began to receive many more invitations to speak. It was the beginning of what would become countless requests for Frost's presence from organizations, colleges, and universities across the United States over the next forty-eight years of his life. He called his speaking activity "barding around." A bard is another name for a poet.

As he became more experienced at speaking in public, Frost learned to conquer his stage fright. He realized that public speaking was a necessary part of his job if he wanted to be successful.[9] Over time he learned to develop an act, in which he portrayed confidence and charm in order to get through the ordeal of speaking to an audience.

By the fall of 1915, Frost settled into a routine of farming, writing, and speaking engagements. By the next summer he began pulling together poems for his third book, *Mountain Interval,* which was published in November 1916. Its sales were well below those of *North of Boston.* Yet the book includes some of Frost's best work, such as "The Road Not Taken," "Birches," and "The Sound of Trees."

All the while, *North of Boston* continued selling briskly. By 1916 the book had gone through four reprintings and had sold twenty thousand copies.[10] Suddenly Frost found that he was considered one of America's best poets, along with Amy Lowell, Edgar Lee Masters, Carl Sandburg, and Edward A. Robinson.

In November of that year, Frost was elected to the National Institute of Arts and Letters, an organization made up of 250 artists, writers, and composers. Its purpose is to promote literature and the fine arts in the United States.

Frost's reputation soared, and he joined the ranks of America's best poets.

In December 1916, the president of Amherst College, Alexander Meiklejohn, offered Frost a position to teach there. He was asked to teach just three courses: pre-Shakespearian drama, poetry, and freshman writing. This was an unusual proposal, since Frost did not have a college degree. But Meiklejohn was on a mission to attract the best faculty possible to the school. He was also interested in exploring new ways of teaching, and he knew of Frost's reputation for innovative teaching methods.

Frost debated the offer in his mind. He did not want to return to teaching. He was afraid it would take all of his time and creative energy. On the other hand, his farm in Franconia was not doing very well. A teaching position would bring him a steady income.[11] So he accepted and began teaching in January 1917. He moved his family to Amherst, Massachusetts, where they lived in a yellow frame house on Dana Street, close to the campus.

That April, Frost received word of his friend Edward Thomas's death. He had been killed in action while fighting for Great Britain in World War I. Frost was grief-stricken by this loss. He wrote to Thomas's wife, Helen, saying, "He was the bravest and best and dearest man you and I have ever known."[12] Later, Frost wrote a poem for his friend entitled, "To ET."

In the fall of 1917, Frost's teaching load at Amherst was reduced so that he would have more time to write. He only taught one course—advanced composition. In addition, he was allowed to be away from campus as much as he needed to fulfill speaking engagements.

Frost's approach to teaching continued to be rather unconventional for that time. His advanced composition class, for example, had no scheduled time or place to meet. According to the school's course description, "Hours [were to be] arranged at the convenience of the instructor and students."[13] One of his students said that the class was often held at a fraternity house, and might last until midnight.[14]

Frost usually taught sprawled in a chair, from which he would throw out questions for his students to discuss. Then he would guide their comments in different directions, his primary goal being to make them think for themselves. Ever popular with his students, they would often visit him at his home, where he might read or talk about poetry well into the night.

By the spring of 1918, Frost was still frustrated. Even with his light teaching schedule, he did not have enough time to write. He wanted to get back to Franconia to farm and write in an undisturbed environment.[15] "I strain at those bonds [his teaching responsibilities] all the time and of course they only cut deeper the more I strain," he wrote.[16]

President Meiklejohn offered Frost an honorary degree from Amherst if he would teach through the next fall. After that, he would be free of teaching commitments. In return, Frost agreed to stay on at the college for one more year. In the spring of 1918 Amherst bestowed upon Frost his first honorary degree, a master of arts.

In the spring of 1920, Frost resigned his duties at Amherst. By this time his need to get back to writing full time had become too strong to resist. In addition, he had sharp disagreements with President Meiklejohn about how best to run the school.

Free of his responsibilities at Amherst, Frost would publish ten new poems in 1920. They became the foundation for his next book, *New Hampshire.*

Frost named this rustic old Vermont farmhouse Stone House.

Toward the end of that year, the Frosts moved once again. Discouraged by the lack of productivity of the Franconia farm, they decided to look for another property in a more moderate climate.[17] This time, they found a ninety-acre farm near South Shaftsbury, Vermont. It had a rustic, old farmhouse, over one hundred years old. Built of rough-hewn Vermont stone with a slate roof, it had no running water or furnace. Despite the ruggedness of the home itself, Frost liked the place. He thought he would be able to write there.[18] They would call it Stone House.

In 1921 the president of the University of Michigan in Ann Arbor wrote to Frost, offering him what would be a new position there as fellow in the creative arts. He offered Frost $5,000 a year in salary, a very generous amount for relatively little work. Frost would have no teaching responsibilities, but would simply be asked to make himself available as an adviser to students and professors.

Taking the job would mean moving away from New England, which Frost did not want to do.[19] Yet he was intrigued by the idea of working at a large university.[20] He accepted the offer, and the Frosts prepared to pack up and move once again.

A University Fellow

Becoming a fellow at a university means taking a temporary position as part of the university's faculty. Usually a fellow is expected to have light teaching responsibilities and do research in his or her field of expertise.

9

SUCCESS AND TRAGEDY

Frost began his duties as a fellow in creative arts at the University of Michigan in the fall of 1921. As he had no direct teaching responsibilities, he referred to himself as the university's "Idle Fellow."[1]

While there, Frost brought in a variety of nationally known poets to lecture, including Vachel Lindsay, Amy Lowell, and Carl Sandburg. He also gave poetry readings on a regular basis. Frost had an impact on many of the students he came in contact with during his time there. A fellow professor later reflected on Frost's influence, saying, "The periods during which he [Frost] lived here were highlights in the lives of the students he came to know. He not only influenced their writing, but he was a great force for good in their lives."[2]

In May 1923, the new president of Amherst visited

Frost to ask if he would consider coming back there once again. He offered to give Frost a position as poet-in-residence, with responsibility for teaching two courses of his choosing. With Amherst's former president, Alexander Meiklejohn, no longer at the college, along with Frost's longing to return to New England, he accepted the offer. He began again at Amherst in the fall of 1923.

Frost's fourth book, *New Hampshire*, was published in November 1923. It was his first illustrated book, with woodcuts by J. J. Lankes. The book also included one of his most enduring poems, "Stopping By Woods on a Snowy Evening." *New Hampshire* received many favorable reviews.[3] The next year it was judged the best book of poems published in 1923 and awarded the Pulitzer Prize for Poetry when the awards were given in 1924. The Pulitzer Prize had been

Stopping By Woods on a Snowy Evening

Whose woods these are I think I know.
His house is in the village though;
He will not see me stopping here
To watch his woods fill up with snow.

My little horse must think it queer
To stop without a farmhouse near
Between the woods and frozen lake
The darkest evening of the year.

He gives his harness bells a shake
To ask if there is some mistake.
The only other sound's the sweep
Of easy wind and downy flake.

The woods are lovely, dark and deep,
But I have promises to keep,
And miles to go before I sleep,
And miles to go before I sleep.

established in 1917 to award outstanding achievements in drama, literature, music, and journalism. It is one of the highest honors an author can receive. Winning the Pulitzer Prize added to Frost's growing reputation as a national figure.

Frost would stay at Amherst for two school terms, until 1925. That spring, Elinor collapsed from nervous exhaustion. Frost blamed himself for his wife's illness. He felt he had been the cause of too much upheaval in their household over the years. They had no set schedule or routine because of his continual job changes and moves. He knew she wanted and needed a more stable, quiet lifestyle.[4]

Yet, how could he stop? Requests for him to speak, lecture, and read continued to pour in. At the same time, Frost was feeling pressure to get another book of poems published. He was afraid that if he did not publish frequently, his public would forget about him.[5]

In the fall of 1925, Frost returned to the University of Michigan for one final year. The university president offered him a permanent position there as a fellow in letters. He would not have to teach any courses; his main duties would be to write and to conduct seminars.

After only one year, Frost resigned his position there and returned to New England. The president of Amherst College offered him $5,000 to teach for ten weeks each year. He was delighted to accept. That way,

New Hampshire won Frost his first Pulitzer Prize for Poetry. The Pulitzer Prize is one of the highest honors an author can receive.

he could get back home to New England and also be closer to his children.[6]

Frost began at Amherst for the third time in January 1927. He would remain there for almost twelve years. During that time, a relatively stable pattern emerged in Frost's life. He spent part of each year at Amherst teaching and lecturing. The rest of his time was divided between writing and speaking engagements.

In 1928, Frost's fifth book, *West-Running Brook*, was published. It includes "Once by the Pacific," a poem that alludes to his childhood in San Francisco. Reviews of *West-Running Brook* were not very enthusiastic. Some said his poems were more appropriate for an earlier time.[7] But Frost viewed his work differently. He considered each of his poems to be a nugget of truth and stability in a chaotic world.[8]

Also that year, the Frosts, along with their daughter Marjorie, traveled to England to visit friends they had made there fifteen years earlier. Frost used the opportunity to go to Ireland as well, where he met with other writers and had dinner with the famed poet William Butler Yeats, whose poetry he had admired for years.

> **Frost considered each of his poems to be a nugget of truth and stability in a chaotic world.**

Frost also found another farm in 1928, which he was instantly drawn to. Just two miles from Stone House, it included 153 acres, fifty of which were woodlands, while the rest were rolling pastureland. The eighteenth-century home had five rooms and three fireplaces. Frost bought this farm for himself and Elinor. They called it The Gulley. He then gave Stone House to his son, Carol.

The next year Frost's sister, Jeanie, died at the age

Frost on his farm in Vermont.

of fifty-three. By that time she had been living for nine years in the state hospital for the mentally ill in Augusta, Maine.

Throughout the 1920s, Frost did not write very much poetry, and the work he did was not considered to be his best. However, in 1930, a volume of his previous work, called *Collected Poems*, was published. While initial reviews were critical, others followed that were more positive. The book sold very well, appealing to a broad range of people. Frost also received his second Pulitzer Prize for the book.

The year 1930 brought another great honor to Frost. He was elected to the American Academy of Arts and Letters. He had been a member of the National Institute of Arts and Letters since 1916, but this was a higher honor, as this group of only fifty artists was elected from the 250 members of the National Institute.

That fall, the Frost's daughter Marjorie was diagnosed with tuberculosis. To get her the best care possible, they sent her to Mesa Verde Sanitarium, a long-term-care hospital in Boulder, Colorado.

By 1933 Marjorie's health had improved dramatically. She had also fallen in love with an archaeology student at the University of Colorado, Willard E. Fraser. Before long she was planning her wedding for that summer. The Frosts were delighted that their daughter's life now seemed to be moving in a positive direction.[9]

> The year **1930** brought another **great honor. Frost was elected to the** American **Academy of Arts and Letters.**

In March 1934 Marjorie gave birth to the couple's child. But the Frosts soon learned that their daughter's health had been affected by the birth; she became seriously ill with an infection. Robert and Elinor flew to Billings, Montana, to be with their daughter and help attend to her care. But her condition only got worse. Desperate, they had her flown to the Mayo Clinic in Rochester, Minnesota. The doctors there could do nothing for her. In a telegram Frost sent to a friend on April 12, he wrote, "Nothing good to tell or predict. Marjorie very low. All we have is hope."[10] Unfortunately, hope was not enough. Marjorie died on May 2, 1934.

The Frosts were beside themselves with grief and anguish over the loss of their daughter. Frost wrote to his friend Louis Untermeyer, "Well, the blow has fallen. The noblest of us all is dead and has taken our hearts out of the world with her."[11] Elinor could not write of her grief at first. But after several months, she wrote to a friend, "She [Marjorie] wanted to live so badly. . . . I long to die myself and be relieved of the pain that I feel for her sake."[12]

That November, Elinor suffered a heart attack. At the advice of her doctor, the Frosts planned to spend the winter months of 1934–1935 in Florida. Their doctor thought that the weather there might be better for Frost, as well as for his wife. They traveled to Key West, which was a very rustic and undeveloped place at that time. All the while, Elinor's health remained fragile.

By March 1936, Frost had been selected by

Harvard as the Charles Eliot Norton Professor of Poetry. He would give six lectures, to be published by the Harvard University Press. It was a great honor, and with his acceptance, Frost felt some self-satisfaction to be returning to Harvard in glory after having left there with his education uncompleted thirty-seven years earlier.[13]

Frost's Harvard lectures were a huge success. He filled the lecture hall each evening he presented, speaking to over one thousand listeners at each session. Some showed up as much as four hours early to get a good seat.

In June 1936, Frost's next book, *A Further Range*, was published. It was also selected as a Book-of-the-Month-Club choice. That meant that Frost could expect sales of at least fifty thousand copies, along with substantial royalties. Although a number of his friends gave the book positive reviews, some were unfavorable. One reviewer said he was tired of poems about New England. Others said Frost's poems were not fresh anymore.[14]

The negative reviews threw Frost into a deep depression. They struck at one of his deepest fears— that he would descend into creative decline.[15] In response, he canceled most of his scheduled lectures and readings for late summer and early fall of 1936.

After about four months, Frost slowly began to pull himself together. In recognition of his long

Colleges and universities competed for Frost's presence on their faculty.

working relationship with Henry Holt and Company, the publishing house compiled a special book, titled *Recognition of Robert Frost: Twenty-fifth Anniversary,* which was published in 1937. It contained selected poems, along with critical reviews and essays. The opening essay, "The Permanence of Robert Frost," was written by the critic and poet Mark Van Doren. In it, Van Doren called Frost "a poet of and for the world."[16] The book contained a number of other essays as well, stressing Frost's importance in American literature.

In May 1937, Frost received his third Pulitzer Prize, this time for *A Further Range.* The book sold very well. In June of that year he was also awarded an honorary doctorate of letters from Harvard University.

In the winter of 1938, Frost took Elinor back to Florida, as her health continued to be poor. They stayed in Gainesville, sharing a house they rented with their daughter Lesley. Carol and his family joined them too, renting a house nearby.

That spring, Elinor suddenly collapsed from the effects of yet another heart attack. Her condition was so fragile she could not be moved to a hospital, so a doctor attended to her at the house. Frost was so upset about his wife's condition that the doctor had to ban him from Elinor's room. Over the next two days she suffered several more heart attacks that weakened her further. Elinor Frost died on March 20, 1938.

10
AMERICA'S POET

With Elinor's death, Frost lost his first and only love. They had been married for forty-three years, throughout which Elinor had stood by her husband in good times and bad. She had also been his personal sounding board for his poetry. He considered her a better poet than he was, and often used her suggestions and advice when writing.

Throughout their marriage, Frost had been totally devoted to Elinor. He said that he had written all of his poems with her in mind.[1] The loss of his wife grieved him more than he thought possible.[2]

Yet Frost finally began to emerge from his grief and depression. He decided that staying busy would be the best way to combat his loneliness.[3] He also got a black-and-white Border collie, whom he named Gillie, to help keep him company.

Frost resigned from Amherst in 1938. He could not bear to live in the house he and Elinor had shared on Sunset Avenue, with all the memories it held. He returned to Stone House in South Shaftsbury to stay with Carol and his family for a while.

That summer, Kay Morrison offered to fill in for Elinor by acting as Frost's secretary. She had long admired his work, and he enjoyed her company very much. She was intelligent and not intimidated by the aging poet's brilliance.[4]

Kay's husband, Ted, taught English at Harvard and directed the Bread Loaf Writers' Conferences in Ripton, Vermont. Since 1926, Frost had been involved with the conference, which he helped develop.

Frost accepted Kay's offer, and it was the beginning of a relationship that would last the rest of his life. He lived with or near the Morrisons from that point on, and he became like an uncle to the Morrison children.[5] That summer, the company of the Morrisons, along with the intellectual stimulation and attention he received at the Bread Loaf Writers' Conference, began to revive Frost's spirits.

In January 1939, Frost was awarded a Gold Medal for "distinguished work in poetry" by the National Institute of Arts and Letters. It was their highest award, given to honor a writer's body of work. Also that year, Holt published a selection of Frost's earlier poems in a book called *Collected Poems*. At the request of his editor, Frost wrote the book's preface, "The Figure a Poem Makes," giving his views on the writing of poetry.

That summer, Frost bought a farm in Ripton, Vermont, which would become his summer home. It was called the Homer Noble farm for its former owners. With almost three hundred acres, the property was located in the midst of the Green Mountain National Forest. Secluded at the end of a half-mile-long gravel drive, the property included a small farmhouse and a cabin. Frost offered the main house to the Morrison family to rent each summer, while he took the cabin. Kay helped him by cooking his meals and assisting him with his correspondence.

In the fall of 1939, Frost took a position at Harvard that had been created especially for him—the Ralph Waldo Emerson Fellowship in Poetry. He taught one course in poetry and again developed a loyal following among his students.[6] He would teach at Harvard for the next three years.

A Tranquil Life

Even in his later years, Frost continued his habit of staying up late at night and getting up around noon each day. After breakfasting on milk and a raw egg, he often spent his afternoons hiking around his Ripton property, always on the lookout for new varieties of wildflowers and other plants. He ate dinner with the Morrisons, and enjoyed playing with their two children. In the evenings, from around 10 P.M. to 3 A.M., he would read, write, or just think.

In his work, Frost found refuge from the tragedies of his life.

In 1940, Frost bought five acres of undeveloped land in Coconut Grove, Florida, where he would spend his winters. Over time, he had two small houses built on the property, which he called Pencil Pines.

By this time, his son, Carol, was in a very bad mental state, suffering from deep depression and anxiety. He saw himself as a failure in life, always having to borrow money from his father, and never able to succeed on his own as a farmer or as a poet. He had dealt with those feelings for years, but as time went by, he only got worse.[7]

In October, Carol asked his father to stay with him while his wife, Lillian, was in the hospital. During their time together, Frost and Carol had long talks, with Frost trying to encourage and support his son, hoping to ease his fears and feelings of worthlessness.

From there, Frost returned to his Ripton home, thinking his son was in a better frame of mind.[8] But Carol's emotional state continued to decline. He was also despondent because he thought his wife was going to die. On October 9, Frost got a call from Carol's teenaged son, Prescott, saying that his father had shot and killed himself. Frost reeled from the impact of yet another tragedy in his family. He also felt guilty about his son's death.[9]

Frost's next book, *A Witness Tree*, was published in 1942. It included one of his best-loved poems, "The Gift Outright," which he would recite in 1961 at the inaugural of President John F. Kennedy. Another poem, "The Silken Tent," received special attention as well. One reviewer called it "one of the finest sonnets written in English in this century."[10]

Frost dedicated the book to Kay Morrison. He wrote, "I owe everything in the world to her. She found me in the gutter, hopeless, sick, run down. She bundled me up and carted me to her home and cared for me like a child. . . ."[11]

A Witness Tree received very positive reviews. One, in *Poetry* magazine, said, "Frost has raised perfectly common, seemingly simple, speech to a moving and memorable experience."[12] The book was popular, too, with ten thousand copies sold in less than two months after its publication. In 1943, Frost received an unprecedented fourth Pulitzer Prize for *A Witness Tree*.

That summer, Frost left Harvard for Dartmouth, becoming the George Ticknor Fellow in the Humanities there. With that move, he had come full circle, back to his roots at Dartmouth, the school he had walked away from as a student over fifty years before. He would have a light schedule, making himself available to students for conferences on weekends during the fall and spring. He also taught one course at Dartmouth, which mainly consisted of him talking about whatever was on his mind at the time—politics, poetry, philosophy, farming, and so forth. In an interview, a Darmouth administrator at the time recognized the value Frost added to the school's reputation: "Frost was the only poet most Americans had ever heard of. They read his work, and admired him. He was an institution. . . ."[13] Frost would stay at Dartmouth for the next six years.

> **In 1943, Frost received an unprecedented fourth Pulitzer Prize for *A Witness Tree.***

In 1945, Frost decided to tackle the philosophical issue of why God allows humans to suffer, by writing his first play, *A Masque of Reason*. As background, he studied the book of Job in the Bible, which is about a good man who is beset

Frost plays a game of pick-up sticks with his daughter Lesley and granddaughters Elinor and Lesley Lee Francis. Gillie the dog naps contently alongside them.

by many misfortunes. A second play followed, *A Masque of Mercy*, based on the biblical account of Jonah.

In 1947, his next book, *Steeple Bush*, was published. While not considered Frost's finest work, it received many positive reviews from critics who respected the poet's vast body of work.[14]

In the meantime, Frost's daughter Irma was having struggles of her own. Her marriage of twenty years was falling apart. In addition, she had long dealt with the same kinds of mental difficulties—depression and anxiety—that had plagued the Frost family. By 1948, Irma was no longer able to care for herself. That year, Frost had his daughter committed to the New Hampshire State Mental Hospital in Concord.

His next book, *Collected Poems*, was published in 1949. Also that year, Frost left Dartmouth to return once again to Amherst as the Simpson Fellowship Lecturer. For that position, he agreed to lecture on campus for two weeks in the spring and two more weeks in the fall. His appointment was made for life.

For his seventy-sixth birthday, in 1950, Frost was honored by the United States Senate, which passed a unanimous resolution to "extend him the felicitations of the Nation which he has served so well."[15]

In 1957 Frost flew to England to receive honorary degrees from Oxford and Cambridge Universities. He was delighted with the dual tribute, writing, "Few things could give me the pleasure of such an honor from the country ('half my own') that published my very first book. I shall look at it as a rounding out that we seldom get except in story books and none too often there."[16] Besides receiving the honorary degrees, his time in England was filled with interviews, dinners, and receptions in his honor, along with ample press coverage.

Frost celebrated his eighty-fifth birthday in 1959.

In late 1958, Frost was appointed poetry consultant at the Library of Congress in Washington, D.C. Also that year, he received the Emerson-Thoreau Medal from the American Academy of Arts and Sciences.

In November 1960, John F. Kennedy won the presidential election and Frost recited his poem "The Gift Outright" at the inauguration ceremony the following January. His participation in the inauguration further boosted his fame. By this time he was recognized wherever he went, and people often asked for his autograph.

In the Clearing, published in 1962, would be Frost's last book of poems. It was published on his eighty-eighth birthday, the same day he was presented with the Congressional Gold Medal by President Kennedy. *In the Clearing* immediately became a best seller. Over time, it sold sixty thousand copies. Later that year, Frost traveled to the Soviet Union as part of a literary exchange. Throughout his visit, he was well received by enthusiastic Soviet audiences.

In the Clearing, Frost's last book of poems, was published on his eighty-eighth birthday and immediately became a best seller.

By the time he returned home from the Soviet Union, Frost was exhausted;

at eighty-eight, his health was finally catching up with him. His last public reading was in December 1962 at Boston's Ford Forum. Shortly after that, he was admitted to Boston's Peter Bent Brigham Hospital where he had surgery to remove cancerous tissue. While recuperating, Frost suffered a pulmonary embolism—the blockage of a blood vessel in the lungs. He died in his sleep on January 29, 1963.

America's poet drew his inspiration from nature.

Robert Frost had become, and remains, an American icon, a symbol for his country with poetry that dignified rural America, the ordinary person, and working the land. But Frost's life story was also one of perseverance despite all odds. In an interview toward the end of his life, Frost reflected on his life choices. He said, "All or nothing, that is how I wanted it, how I have lived."[17] He risked everything for his passion—poetry—and his risk paid off.

> **"All or nothing, that is how I wanted it, how I have lived."**

In March 1962, for Frost's eighty-eighth birthday, his publisher, by that time renamed Holt, Rinehart and Winston, had hosted a dinner for him at the Pan-American Building in Washington, D.C. One of the speakers honoring Frost that night was Adlai Stevenson, the United States ambassador to the United Nations. He said, "In Robert Frost, I daresay the American people have found their poet, their seer, their singer—in short, their bard."[18] Indeed, they had.

CHRONOLOGY

Robert Lee Frost is born March 26 in San Francisco, California.	**1874**
Robert's father, William Prescott Frost Jr. dies of tuberculosis. Mrs. Frost takes Robert and his younger sister, Jeanie, to live in Massachusetts.	**1885**
Begins high school at Lawrence High School in Massachusetts.	**1888**
Graduates as co-valedictorian from Lawrence High School. Enters Dartmouth College in the fall, and quits before the end of the first semester.	**1892**
"My Butterfly: An Elegy" becomes Frost's first published poem, appearing in *The Independent* magazine.	**1894**
Marries Elinor Miriam White.	**1895**
First child, Elliott, is born.	**1896**
Enters Harvard College.	**1897**
Discontinues studies at Harvard for health reasons. Second child, Lesley, is born.	**1899**
Moves to Derry, New Hampshire, to farm. Son, Elliott, dies of cholera. Belle Frost dies of cancer.	**1900**
Grandfather dies, willing Derry Farm to Frost, along with a yearly allowance.	**1901**

1902	Son Carol is born.
1903	Daughter Irma is born.
1905	Daughter Marjorie is born.
1906	Begins teaching at Pinkerton Academy in Derry, New Hampshire.
1911	Begins teaching at New Hampshire State Normal School.
1912	Moves to England. David Nutt and Company accepts manuscript for *A Boy's Will.*
1913	*A Boy's Will* is published and is reviewed by Ezra Pound.
1914	*North of Boston* is published.
1915	Frost and family return to the United States. Move to Franconia, New Hampshire, farm.
1916	*Mountain Interval* is published. Frost is elected to the National Institute of Arts and Letters.
1917	Begins teaching at Amherst College, Amherst, Massachusetts.
1918	Receives first honorary degree, master of arts, from Amherst College.
1920	Resigns from Amherst College. Moves to South Shaftsbury, Vermont.
1921	Begins at University of Michigan, Ann Arbor, as Fellow in Creative Arts.

New Hampshire is published. Frost returns to Amherst College to teach.	**1923**
Receives the Pulitzer Prize for *New Hampshire*.	**1924**
Returns to the University of Michigan as Fellow in Letters.	**1925**
Returns to Amherst College to teach.	**1927**
West-Running Brook is published.	**1928**
Collected Poems is published. Frost is elected to the American Academy of Arts and Letters.	**1930**
Receives Pulitzer Prize for *Collected Poems*.	**1931**
Daughter Marjorie dies.	**1934**
Selected as Charles Eliot Norton Professor of Poetry, Harvard University. *A Further Range* is published.	**1936**
Receives Pulitzer Prize for *A Further Range*.	**1937**
Wife, Elinor, dies. Frost resigns from Amherst College.	**1938**
Awarded Gold Medal for Poetry by the National Institute of Arts and Letters. *Collected Poems* is published. Frost receives appointment as Ralph Waldo Emerson Fellow in Poetry at Harvard University.	**1939**
Son, Carol, dies of self-inflicted gunshot wound.	**1940**

1941   Awarded Gold Medal by the Poetry Society of America.

1942   *A Witness Tree* is published.

1943   Receives Pulitzer Prize for *A Witness Tree*. Is appointed George Ticknor Fellow in the Humanities at Dartmouth College.

1945   *A Masque of Reason* is published.

1947   *Steeple Bush* and *A Masque of Mercy* are published.

1949   *Collected Poems* is published. Receives life appointment as Simpson Lecturer in Literature, Amherst College.

1950   U.S. Senate adopts resolution honoring Frost.

1957   Receives Honorary Doctor of Letters from Oxford and Cambridge Universities.

1958   Appointed Consultant in Poetry at the Library of Congress.

1960   Receives Congressional Gold Medal authorized by President Dwight D. Eisenhower.

1961   Participates in the inaugural ceremonies for President John F. Kennedy.

1962   *In the Clearing* is published. President Kennedy presents Frost with the Congresssional Gold Medal.

1963   Frost dies on January 29 in Boston.

WORKS BY ROBERT FROST

A Boy's Will, 1913

North of Boston, 1914

Mountain Interval, 1916

New Hampshire, 1923

West-Running Brook, 1928

Collected Poems, 1930

A Further Range, 1936

Collected Poems, 1939

A Witness Tree, 1942

A Masque of Reason, 1945

A Masque of Mercy, 1947

Steeple Bush, 1947

Collected Poems, 1949

In the Clearing, 1962

CHAPTER NOTES

Chapter 1. A Gift for the Nation

1. William H. Pritchard, *Frost: A Literary Life Reconsidered* (New York: Oxford University Press, 1984), p. 253.

2. Lawrance Thompson and R. H. Winnick; Edward Connery Lathem, ed., *Robert Frost* (New York: Holt, Rinehart and Winston, 1981), p. 480.

3. Pritchard, p. 254.

4. Thompson, p. 481.

5. Ibid., p. 481.

6. Jay Parini, *Robert Frost: A Life* (New York: Henry Holt and Company, Inc., 1999), p. 335.

7. Ibid., p. 415.

8. "Frost's Poem Wins Hearts at Inaugural," *Washington Post*, January 21, 1961, p. 8.

Chapter 2. The Wild West

1. Elizabeth Shepley Sergeant, *Robert Frost, The Trial by Existence* (New York: Holt, Rinehart and Winston, 1960), p. 7.

2. Lawrance Thompson and R. H. Winnick; Edward Connery Lathem, ed., *Robert Frost* (New York: Holt, Rinehart and Winston, 1981), p. 5.

3. Louis Mertins, *Robert Frost, Life and Talks-Walking* (Norman, Oklahoma: University of Oklahoma Press, 1965), p. 9.

4. Ibid., p. 7.

5. Thompson, p. 13.

6. Shepley Sergeant, p. 7.

7. Thompson, p. 14.

8. Mertins, p. 11.

9. Ibid.

10. Thompson, p. 20.

11. Shepley Sergeant, p. 15.

Chapter 3. A Change of Scenery

1. Jay Parini, *Robert Frost: A Life* (New York: Henry Holt and Company, Inc., 1999), p. 20.

2. Lawrance Thompson and R. H. Winnick; Edward Connery Lathem, ed., *Robert Frost* (New York: Holt, Rinehart and Winston, 1981), p. 31.

3. Ibid., p. 36.

4. Louis Mertins, *Robert Frost, Life and Talks-Walking* (Norman, Oklahoma: University of Oklahoma Press, 1965), p. 39.

5. Gorham Munson, *Making Poems for America: Robert Frost* (Chicago: F. E. Compton & Co., 1962), p. 24.

6. Thompson, p. 37.

7. Ibid., p. 39.

8. Munson, p. 24.

9. Thompson, p. 42.

10. Ibid., p. 47.

11. Mertins, p. 44.

12. Elizabeth Shepley Sergeant, *Robert Frost, The Trial by Existence* (New York: Holt, Rinehart and Winston, 1960), p. 22.

13. Parini, p. 28.

14. Shepley Sergeant, p. 26.

15. Thompson, p. 63.

Chapter 4. Dead Ends

1. Daniel Smythe, *Robert Frost Speaks* (New York: Twayne Publishers, Inc., 1964), p. 18.

2. Gorham Munson, *Making Poems for America: Robert Frost* (Chicago: F. E. Compton & Co., 1962), pp. 32–33.

3. Lawrance Thompson and R. H. Winnick; Edward Connery Lathem, ed., *Robert Frost* (New York: Holt, Rinehart and Winston, 1981), p. 69.

4. Jay Parini, *Robert Frost: A Life* (New York: Henry Holt and Company, Inc., 1999), p. 36.

5. Ibid., p. 37.

6. Lawrance Thompson, ed., *Selected Letters of Robert Frost* (New York: Holt, Rinehart and Winston, 1964), p. 167.

7. Louis Mertins, *Robert Frost, Life and Talks-Walking* (Norman, Oklahoma: University of Oklahoma Press, 1965), p. 50.

8. Munson, p. 33.

9. Elizabeth Shepley Sergeant, *Robert Frost, The Trial by Existence* (New York: Holt, Rinehart and Winston, 1960), p. 30.

10. Stanley Burnshaw, *Robert Frost Himself* (New York: George Braziller, 1986), p. 255.

11. Thompson, p. 73.

12. Parini, p. 40.

13. Thompson, pp. 73–74.

14. Ibid., p. 74.

15. Ibid., p. 75.

Chapter 5. A Slow Start

1. Louis Mertins, *Robert Frost, Life and Talks-Walking* (Norman, Oklahoma: University of Oklahoma Press, 1965), p. 57.

2. Jay Parini, *Robert Frost: A Life* (New York: Henry Holt and Company, Inc., 1999), p. 42.

3. Elizabeth Shepley Sergeant, *Robert Frost, The Trial by Existence* (New York: Holt, Rinehart and Winston, 1960), p. 34.

4. Lea Newman, *Robert Frost: The People, Places, and Stories Behind His New England Poetry* (Shelburne, VT: The New England Press, Inc., 2000), p. 2.

5. Parini, p. 46.

6. Newman, p. 3.

7. Shepley Sergeant, p. 35.

8. Lawrance Thompson, ed., *Selected Letters of Robert Frost* (New York: Holt, Rinehart and Winston, 1964), p. 19.

9. Ibid., p. 23.

10. Parini, p. 46.

11. Mertins, p. 56.

12. Lawrance Thompson and R. H. Winnick; Edward Connery Lathem, ed., *Robert Frost* (New York: Holt, Rinehart and Winston, 1981), p. 75.

13. Ibid., p. 76.

14. Shepley Sergeant, p. 42.

15. Parini, p. 47.

16. Gorham Munson, *Making Poems for America: Robert Frost* (Chicago: F. C. Compton & Co., 1962), p. 38.

17. William H. Pritchard, *Frost: A Literary Life Reconsidered* (New York: Oxford University Press, 1984), p. 5.

18. Thompson, p. 83.

19. Mertins, pp. 51–52.

20. Parini, p. 51.

21. Thompson, p. 95.

Chapter 6. Difficult Circumstances

1. William H. Pritchard, *Frost: A Literary Life Reconsidered* (New York: Oxford University Press, 1984), p. 47.

2. Ibid., p. 52.

3. Lawrance Thompson and R. H. Winnick; Edward Connery Lathem, ed., *Robert Frost* (New York: Holt, Rinehart and Winston, 1981), p 111.

4. Jay Parini, *Robert Frost: A Life* (New York: Henry Holt and Company, Inc., 1999), p. 60.

5. Thompson, p. 113.

6. Pritchard, p. 54.

7. Parini, p., 68.

8. Lea Newman, *Robert Frost: The People, Places, and Stories Behind His New England Poetry* (Shelburne, VT: The New England Press, Inc., 2000), p. 81.

9. Ibid., p. 97.

10. Louis Mertins, *Robert Frost, Life and Talks-Walking* (Norman, Oklahoma: University of Oklahoma Press, 1965), p. 65.

11. Ibid., p. 72.

12. Parini, p. 91.

13. Mertins, p. 64.

14. Margaret Bartlett Anderson, Robert Frost, and John Bartlett, *The Record of a Friendship* (New York: Holt, Rinehart and Winston, 1963), p. 5.

15. Mertins, p. 78.

16. Lesley Frost, *New Hampshire's Child* (Albany, New York: State University of New York Press, 1969), Introduction, p. 3.

17. Elizabeth Shepley Sergeant, *Robert Frost, The Trial by Existence* (New York: Holt, Rinehart and Winston, 1960), p. 80.

18. Mertins, p. 89.

19. Ibid., p. 65.

20. Anderson, p. 22.

21. Shepley Sergeant, p. 67.

22. Anderson, p. 9.

23. Pritchard, p. 79.

24. Parini, p. 95.

25. Anderson, p. 11.

26. Shepley Sergeant, p. 84.

27. Ibid., p. 69.

Chapter 7. Turning Point

1. Elizabeth Shepley Sergeant, *Robert Frost, The Trial by Existence* (New York: Holt, Rinehart and Winston, 1960), p. 96.

2. Louis Mertins, *Robert Frost, Life and Talks-Walking* (Norman, Oklahoma: University of Oklahoma Press, 1965), p. 108.

3. Gorham Munson, *Making Poems for America: Robert Frost* (Chicago: F. E. Compton & Co., 1962), pp. 89–90.

4. Shepley Sergeant, p. 112.

5. Mertins, p. 136.

6. William H. Pritchard, *Frost: A Literary Life Reconsidered* (New York: Oxford University Press, 1984), p. 77.

7. Mertins, p. 197.

8. Jay Parini, *Robert Frost: A Life* (New York: Henry Holt and Company, Inc., 1999), p.145.

9. Shepley Sergeant, p. 129.

10. Mertins, p. 127.

11. Munson, p. 96.

12. Helen Thomas, with Myfanwy Thomas, *Under Storm's Wing* (London: Paladin Grafton Books, 1990), p. 229.

13. Ibid.

14. Lawrance Thompson, ed., *Selected Letters of Robert Frost* (New York: Holt, Rinehart and Winston, 1964), p. 220.

15. Parini, pp. 155–156.

16. Thompson, p. 152.

Chapter 8. Moving Forward

1. Jay Parini, *Robert Frost: A Life* (New York: Henry Holt and Company, Inc., 1999), p. 158.

2. Louis Mertins, *Robert Frost, Life and Talks-Walking* (Norman, Oklahoma: University of Oklahoma Press, 1965), p. 140.

3. Ibid.

4. Elizabeth Shepley Sergeant, *Robert Frost, The Trial by Existence* (New York: Holt, Rinehart and Winston, 1960), p. 152.

5. Mertins, p. 141.

6. Lawrance Thompson and R. H. Winnick; Edward Connery Lathem, ed., *Robert Frost* (New York: Holt, Rinehart and Winston, 1981), p. 208.

7. Parini, p. 106.

8. Thompson, p. 227.

9. Ibid.

10. Ibid., p. 171.

11. Thompson, pp. 232–233.

12. Lawrance Thompson, ed., *Selected Letters of Robert Frost* (New York: Holt, Rinehart and Winston, 1964), p. 216.

13. William H. Pritchard, *Frost: A Literary Life Reconsidered* (New York: Oxford University Press, 1984), p. 129.

14. Ibid., p. 130.

15. Parini, p. 191.

16. Pritchard, p.132.

17. Thompson, p. 258.

18. Parini, p. 195.

19. Ibid., p. 205.

20. Pritchard, p. 140.

Chapter 9. Success and Tragedy

1. Elizabeth Shepley Sergeant, *Robert Frost, The Trial by Existence* (New York: Holt, Rinehart and Winston, 1960), p. 240.

2. Ibid., p. 246.

3. Jay Parini, *Robert Frost: A Life* (New York: Henry Holt and Company, Inc., 1999), p. 227.

4. Ibid., p. 220.

5. Gorham Munson, *Making Poems for America: Robert Frost* (Chicago: F. E. Compton & Co., 1962), p. 166.

6. Lawrance Thompson and R. H. Winnick; Edward Connery Lathem, ed., *Robert Frost* (New York: Holt, Rinehart and Winston, 1981), p. 308.

7. Parini, p. 267.

8. Ibid.

9. Parini, pp. 277–278.

10. Shepley Sergeant, p. 330.

11. Louis Untermeyer, *The Letters of Robert Frost to Louis Untermeyer* (New York: Holt, Rinehart and Winston, 1963), p. 241.

12. Lawrance Thompson, ed., *Selected Letters of Robert Frost* (New York: Holt, Rinehart and Winston, 1964), p. 412.

13. Shepley Sergeant, p. 347.

14. Parini, p. 306.

15. Munson, p. 166.

16. Parini, p. 308.

Chapter 10. America's Poet

1. Jay Parini, *Robert Frost: A Life* (New York: Henry Holt and Company, Inc., 1999), p. 445.

2. Sandra L. Katz, *Elinor Frost: A Poet's Wife* (Westfield, Massachusetts: Institute for Massachusetts Studies, Westfield State College, 1988), p. 157.

3. Parini, p. 313.

4. Ibid., p. 303.

5. Ibid., p. 315.

6. Elizabeth Shepley Sergeant, *Robert Frost, The Trial by Existence* (New York: Holt, Rinehart and Winston, 1960), p. 377.

7. Parini, p. 331.

8. Shepley Sergeant, p. 368.

9. Parini, p. 332.

10. Parini, p. 320.

11. Louis Mertins, *Robert Frost, Life and Talks-Walking* (Norman, Oklahoma: University of Oklahoma Press, 1965), p. 233.

12. Parini, p. 343.

13. Ibid., p. 348.

14. Ibid., pp. 369–370.

15. Lawrance Thompson and R. H. Winnick; Edward Connery Lathem, ed., *Robert Frost* (New York: Holt, Rinehart and Winston, 1981), p. 451.

16. Lawrance Thompson, ed., *Selected Letters of Robert Frost* (New York: Holt, Rinehart and Winston, 1964), pp. 564–565.

17. Parini, p. 442.

18. Gorham Munson, *Making Poems for America: Robert Frost* (Chicago: F. E. Compton & Co., 1962), p. 190.

FURTHER READING

Books

Bloom, Harold, ed. *Robert Frost.* Broomall, Penn.: Chelsea House Publishers, 2002.

Bober, Natalie S. *A Restless Spirit: The Story of Robert Frost.* New York: Henry Holt and Company, 1999.

DeFusco, Andrea, ed. *Readings on Robert Frost.* San Diego, California: Greenhaven Press, Inc., 1999.

Frost, Robert, and Louis Untermeyer. *Road Not Taken: An Introduction to Robert Frost.* New York: Henry Holt and Company, 1995.

Schmidt, Gary D., ed. *Poetry for Young People: Robert Frost.* New York: Sterling Publishing Company, Inc., 1994.

Audio Recording

Frost, Robert. *Voice of the Poet.* Caedmon, 2003.

INTERNET ADDRESSES

Robert Frost, Life and Career
<http://www.english.uiuc.edu/maps/poets/a_f/
 frost/life.htm>

The Friends of Robert Frost
<http://www.frostfriends.org/>

INDEX

Page numbers for photographs are in **boldface** type.